VGM Opportuni

OPPORTUNITIES IN BROADCASTING CAREERS

Elmo I. Ellis

Foreword by
E. Culpepper Clark
Dean, College of Communication and Information Sciences
The University of Alabama

VGM Career Horizons
NTC/Contemporary Publishing Group

Library of Congress Cataloging-in-Publication Data

Ellis, Elmo Israel.
   Opportunities in broadcasting careers / Elmo Ellis. — Rev. ed.
      p. cm. — (VGM opportunities series)
   Rev. ed. of: Opportunities in broadcasting. 1981.
   Includes bibliographical references (p.).
   ISBN 0-8442-6467-9. — ISBN 0-8442-6468-7 (pbk.)
   1. Broadcasting—Vocational guidance. I. Ellis, Elmo Israel.
Opportunities in broadcasting. II. Title. III. Series.
HE8689.6.E43 1998
384.54'023'73—dc21   98-17619
                                                                                          CIP

Cover photo credits:
Top left, courtesy WBEZ 91.5 FM, Chicago (photograph of Gretchen Helfrich by Michael Lipman); top right, courtesy Elmhurst College, Elmhurst, Illinois; bottom left, courtesy WBEZ 91.5 FM, Chicago (photograph of reporter Jody Becker, left, and audio supervisor Mary Gaffney, right, by Michael Lipman); bottom right, courtesy the Medill School of Journalism, Northwestern University.

Published by VGM Career Horizons
A division of NTC/Contemporary Publishing Group, Inc.
4255 West Touhy Avenue, Lincolnwood (Chicago), Illinois 60646-1975 U.S.A.
Copyright © 1999 by NTC/Contemporary Publishing Group, Inc.
All rights reserved. No part of this book may be reproduced, stored in a retrieval system, or transmitted in any form or by any means, electronic, mechanical, photocopying, recording, or otherwise, without the prior permission of NTC/Contemporary Publishing Group, Inc.
Printed in the United States of America
International Standard Book Number: 0-8442-6467-9 (cloth)
                                                            0-8442-6468-7(paper)
18   17   16   15   14   13   12   11   10   9   8   7   6   5   4   3   2   1

CONTENTS

About the Author vi
Foreword viii
Acknowledgments x

1. **The New World of Broadcasting** 1
   The communication challenge. The big broadcasting picture. New media era. Electronic narrowcasting. Importance of computer skills. Opportunity and responsibility.

2. **Overview of Electronic Communication** 7
   The birth of broadcasting. Radio growth and regulation. The Communications Act of 1934. AM broadcasting. FM radio. Stereo broadcasting. Development of television. The Telecommunications Act of 1996. Commercial broadcasting in the United States. Electronic media convergence. You and digital technology.

3. **Broadcasting and Narrowcasting in the United States and Canada** 17
   The broadcasting job market. Television in America. Radio resurgence. U.S. cable TV. DBS. Interactive narrowcasting. ISDN. Public broadcasting. Licensed low-power narrowcasting. Unlicensed low-power narrowcasting. Electronic media in Canada. Job hunting in Canada.

4. **You and Electronic Media** 34
   Weighing your media options. Ask the professor. Valuable communication qualities. Job satisfaction. Giving the public what it wants. Electronic media career test.

5. **Preparing for a Career in Electronic Media** 43
   Develop communication skills. What management wants. Need for technical talent. Versatility is valuable. Education. How to get that first job. Resumes and software. The video resume. Licensing. Job hunting tips. Pathway to promotion.

6. **Electronic Media—Rewards and Benefits** 54
   The employment outlook. Working conditions. Money matters.

7. **Radio Jobs** 63
   Group and niche programming. Automation and syndication. Dollars and sense. Programming and production. Disk jockeys and drive-time talent. General announcers. Morning-drive radio salaries. Superstars. Sales. Marketing, promotion, and publicity. Research. Management and administration. Traffic. Engineering. Office service jobs. Combo and part-time jobs. Network jobs.

8. **Jobs in Television and Cable** 77
   Opportunity and responsibility. Program and production jobs. Television personalities. Marketing, promotion, and research jobs. Sales jobs. Management and administrative jobs. Engineering jobs. Network television jobs. Cable TV employment.

9. **Electronic News Careers**...............................90
   Television news. Radio news. Radio news outsourcing. Cable news. Multimedia journalists. Business news jobs. Electronic tabloids. Global news jobs. Newspaper websites. Sportscasting. Career advice from news experts.

10. **Internet Broadcasting** 103
    Internet employment. High-tech scholars. Website business. On-line entrepreneurs. Electronic job finders. Internet Q and A.

Contents v

11. Nonbroadcast Video Systems.......................... 111
Video systems—big business. Video systems jobs. Video production. Video production jobs. Video postproduction jobs.

12. Broadcast-Related Jobs 117
Sales representatives. Advertising agencies. Public relations. Public information. Freelance talent. Syndicated program services. Voice of America. Uncle Sam's radio-TV. "Free" radio. Nonprofit organizations.

13. Jobs for Women and Minorities 125
The minority success route. Gender salary comparison. Minority broadcast ownership. Broadcap. New opportunities. Minority voices and choices. Female role models.

14. The Multimedia Future 134
The changing workplace. Narrowing the focus. What's on the horizon? Digital television. Digital radio. Megachannel television. Satellite prospects. Tomorrow's intermedia world. Outlook for students. A final word.

Appendix A: Scholarships, Grants, and Loans............... 141

Appendix B: Suggested Reading 146

ABOUT THE AUTHOR

Elmo Ellis is widely recognized as one of the most innovative figures in the history of broadcasting. During a lengthy and distinguished career, spanning more than five decades, he originated many types of local and network programs that are now commonly seen and heard on television and radio.

This vice president (emeritus) of Cox Broadcasting Corp., has held programming, production, promotion, public relations, and general management positions and offered one of the country's first courses in TV writing and production at Emory University. He also has taught TV and radio classes at Georgia State and Oglethorpe Universities and often lectures at other schools and colleges. Students frequently seek his advice regarding careers in broadcasting.

As television grew in popularity and radio declined, Ellis wrote articles and delivered speeches about "How to Remove the Rust from Radio." The campaign succeeded in reviving nationwide interest in radio listening, and he won a Peabody award. Over the years he has received hundreds of other national and international awards for programming, civic contributions, and broadcasting leadership.

During the celebration of Radio's diamond anniversary, *Radio INK* magazine paid tribute to Ellis as one of seventy-five legendary broadcasters who have exerted "a distinctive and major impact" on the industry.

He has served as chairman of the Radio Advertising Bureau, the National FM Radio Broadcasters Association, the NAB Radio Code Board, and the NBC Radio Affiliates. He has been president of the

Georgia Association of Broadcasters, Georgia AP News Broadcasters, and the Society of Professional Journalists.

A strong supporter of broadcast education, Ellis is a trustee of Oglethorpe University and a broadcasting advisory board member at Emory University and the University of Alabama.

Holder of three collegiate degrees, and a Phi Beta Kappa key, his books and articles have been published in the United States, Japan, Australia, Canada, and other countries. He is prominently listed in *Who's Who* and continues to share his knowledge and experience as an author, media consultant, public speaker, and syndicated newspaper columnist.

FOREWORD

As the multimedia universe continues to grow and change, all institutions and individuals are being challenged to adapt to new methods of personalized, interactive communication. Conventional analog radio, TV, and cable are being integrated into new forms of digital broadcasting and narrowcasting. In this explosive age of computerized information systems, we are inventing new careers in electronic media and modernizing old ones.

What a splendid experience it is to explore these many new skyways of communication—and the career opportunities they are creating—with one of the nation's most renowned and respected broadcast professionals. Elmo Ellis is the "Dean" of radio and television journalism in the Southeast and a recognized authority on programming and management practices nationally and internationally.

If you are considering the possibility of becoming a computer-age broadcaster, you will find what you need to know in these pages. What kind of jobs are out there? How much preparation is required? What knowledge and technical skills are most important? How much money can one expect to make? Answers to these and many other questions are presented in a most readable and accessible fashion. Only someone of Ellis's background could speak with such authority and credible ease to those who wish to become twenty-first century communicators.

This manual should be helpful to students in high schools, universities, and technical-community colleges who want to learn about the many job options that electronic media convergence has created, as well as the ones it has eliminated. It is also an excellent handbook for those already in the industry who may wish to explore new opportunities. To anyone else who seeks a better understanding of broadcasting and what it has to offer, I say, read this book!

E. Culpepper Clark, Dean
College of Communication and Information Sciences
The University of Alabama

ACKNOWLEDGMENTS

I am indebted to many broadcasters, educators, and electronic media professionals whose generous contributions of information and advice made possible the writing of this book. They include: James W. Wesley, Jr., former president, Patterson Broadcasting Corp.; Michael McDougald, president, McDougald Broadcasting; Bill Sanders, executive vice president, and Lanny Finch, Georgia Association of Broadcasters; Dr. Loren Ghiglione and Dr. Linda Matthews, Emory University; John Holliman, CNN correspondent; Lynda Stewart, Betsy Stone, and David Scott, Cox Enterprises; Richard Warner, president, What's Up!; Bryan Moffett, Radio-TV News Directors Association; Robert Alter, vice chairman, Cable Television Advertising Bureau; Dr. Barry Sherman, director, Peabody Awards, University of Georgia; Dr. Culpepper Clark, Dean, and Dr. Jennings Bryant, College of Communication, University of Alabama; Pamela S. Beaird, director, financial aid, Oglethorpe University; Richard Ducey, vice president, George Barber, vice president, and Michael D. McKinley, National Association of Broadcasters; Mike Mahone, executive vice president, Radio Advertising Bureau; Bill Israel, website host; and the editors of *Advertising Age* and *Broadcasting & Cable Yearbook*.

Most of all, I owe heartfelt thanks to my beloved wife, Ruth, who gave me unstinting assistance, nourishment, and encouragement during the preparation of this manuscript.

CHAPTER 1

THE NEW WORLD OF BROADCASTING

During most of the twentieth century, radio, television, and cable have been transmitting sights and sounds to millions of passive listeners and viewers. Now new forms of interactive communication are emerging and growing in popularity, allowing members of the audience to participate actively as broadcasters in an expanding, multimedia universe.

A recent computer advertisement posed this question: "What would you call a stereo you can fax on, a CD player you can talk on, and a high-speed modem you can watch movies on?" The versatile machine was described as a "multimedia notebook," combining audio, video, and digital capabilities into a single unit of two-way communication.

This kind of interactive device is able to receive programming from individual radio, television, and cable outlets. It also can exchange typed and aural messages and function as an educator, newspaper, magazine, conversation parlor, music hall, bulletin board, shopping service, bookkeeper, information source, entertainer, playmate for games, and social companion.

Digital technology, satellites, fiber optics, lasers, and other sophisticated equipment have created so many options for viewing, listening, and personal expression, that you may wonder, what will happen to conventional radio and television media. Will they continue to exist and serve the public? The answer is yes, but they are changing with the times and investing heavily in digital devices and interactive programs and services.

There's little doubt that increased emphasis on live, person-to-person communication will impact heavily on established media and place increased responsibility on everyone involved in the free, uncensored exchange of ideas and information. But the good news is that interactive media growth is creating businesses, generating jobs, and sparking creativity. Doors of opportunity are steadily opening for talented journalists, graphic artists, digital specialists, salespeople—all kinds of able communicators.

THE COMMUNICATION CHALLENGE

Communication has made possible the level of civilization that we enjoy today. But the communication process is complicated and often creates more problems than it solves. Whether broadcasting to a multitude or quietly conversing with one person, effective communication requires respectful and sensitive collaboration to achieve comprehension and agreement on the content and meaning of what is being transmitted and received.

To be a competent communicator you should meet these requirements:

1. Understand the various ways that people communicate—accurately and inaccurately, rationally and emotionally, purposefully and unknowingly—with words, signs, symbols, sights, sounds, silence, and mannerisms.
2. Learn how to observe, listen, speak, write, and spell with a high degree of competence, empathy, clarity, and perception.
3. Master the tools of personal and mass communication. Become adept at using state-of-the-art technology.
4. Acquire general and specific knowledge that will enable you to analyze and interpret facts, opinions, and theories.
5. Know how and where to obtain information and how to screen and refine it into useful knowledge.
6. Initiate and maintain a lifelong learning program for personal and professional development that will enable you to meet the constantly changing demands of a communication career.

THE BIG BROADCASTING PICTURE

There are almost 600 million working radios in the United States, more than 5 per household. They can be found in virtually every home, automobile, and place of business. Some 12,200 AM and FM radio stations are on the air, and the FCC continues to issue construction permits for more outlets.

About 1,600 commercial and educational TV stations (VHF and UHF) provide entertainment and information to 99 percent of the nation's households. In addition, there are some 2,000 VHF and UHF low-powered television stations and almost 8,000 FM, VHF, and UHF translators and booster stations.

Seven out of ten homes are linked to cable systems. Nielsen Media Research estimates that family members average watching TV for seven and a half hours a day. Although millions of viewers still watch only local TV stations, a growing number subscribe for cable service to get better picture quality and vastly more program choices.

Approximately 11,800 cable systems serve 65 million subscribers in 34,000 communities. A typical system offers 40 or more channels of news, sitcoms, music, sports, movies, comedy, shopping services, weather, financial reports, pay-TV, and dozens of other video programs.

At least 5,300 cable systems originate local programs and maintain "access" channels for local citizens to perform, voice opinions, and present public service messages. One-fourth of all cable systems solicit and air local advertising. Pay-per-view movies are available on cable systems in every state.

Some 250 wireless cable systems supply video service to millions of rooftop antennas. DBS—Direct Broadcast Satellite companies—beam cable and network choices from outer space to backyard antennas.

Between 1987 and 1997, households with computers more than doubled from 18 to 40 percent. On-line Internet surfers are growing at a comparable rate.

This expansion of digital-based technology is generating billions of dollars in billings for TV, radio, cable, makers of computer hardware and software, and thousands of related businesses. It also is creating many jobs. This should be welcome news for young people who are training for a career in some field of electronic communication.

NEW MEDIA ERA*

Never before have the American people had so much easy access to information or so many simple and economical ways to engage in verbal and visual communication. The capabilities of telephone, telegraph, radio, and television are being transferred to, and absorbed by, new multimedia technology.

"We're at the very earliest stages of the most radical transformation of everything we hear, see, and know," thinks Barry Diller, chairman of the Home Shopping Network. Evidence that this may be an accurate prediction exists in the phenomenal growth of new electronic hardware and its widespread usage in all forms of communication.

Sources: *Broadcasting & Cable,* Dec. 15, 1997. Regis McKenna, "Real Time," Harvard Business School Press, 1997.

Assimilation of this exotic technology is occurring not only rapidly but also relatively smoothly. Whereas it took most of the twentieth century to create the infrastructure of radio, television, and cable, the twenty-first century's network of computers, satellites, ground stations, and fiber optic and wireless facilities is already functioning. Chips on which digitized information is stored sell for a fraction of what they formerly cost, and computers, software, and modems are rapidly becoming more affordable.

The multimedia explosion prompted Dietrich Ratzke, a prominent German journalist and educator, to suggest this analogy: "Had automobiles changed with the same speed as micro-electronics, a midclass car would today travel at 1,000 kilometers per hour, would need only a liter of gas per thousand kilometers, would have enough room for 100 passengers, and would cost about ten dollars."

Every day untold millions of people communicate with each other locally, nationally and internationally, via mass media, and person-to-person. Now new devices have expanded the dimensions of this process and made the playing field wider and potentially more productive for broadcasters, narrowcasters, and personal communicaters.

ELECTRONIC NARROWCASTING

As we move into the twenty-first century, broadcasters are aiming less at mass audiences and more toward viewers and listeners with special interests. Instead of trying to attract the maximum number of people, they are catering to smaller demographic clusters. This change has come about because the American people, who for many years were able to see and hear only a limited menu of programs, personalities, and news services, are no longer restricted in their program choices.

Thanks to new technology and a boom in audiovisual outlets, production, and marketing, it is now possible in most communities to obtain entertainment and information from a multitude of sources, including TV, radio, cable, and computer networks; local television, radio, and cable channels; satellite and wireless companies; and tapes, discs, and cassettes of all kinds, coupled with massive amounts of digital data and services. In addition, much of this vast electronic library is designed to accommodate individual game-playing and competition.

Indeed, the traditional concept of broadcasting to the masses is being supplanted by a new policy of interactive narrowcasting to smaller audiences that share common interests. A typical radio station, for example, plays only one kind of music and caters to a certain age and type of listener. Numerous Internet, TV, radio, and cable programs are designed to appeal to particular economic, social, ethnic, religious, and cultural groups. Some TV newscasts are produced exclusively for schoolchildren.

Many public and private institutions own closed-circuit systems or low-powered video and audio stations, from which they transmit programs by wire, cable, or through the air. All such operations focus on relatively few people.

Pay-per-view sports, movies, and special events constitute another form of narrowcasting. The same is true of armed forces radio and television stations, which are maintained all over the world for the benefit of military personnel. There are websites dedicated to even the most obscure subject matter.

The growth and diversification of media choices should produce an increase in the number and variety of jobs available for electronic communicators.

IMPORTANCE OF COMPUTER SKILLS

All across the county, employers are recruiting on campus for students with computer skills. A nationwide survey of 340 career service offices, conducted by the National Association of Colleges and Employers, indicates that graduates with degrees in computer science, electrical engineering, or information systems are stepping from the classroom into attractive, high-salaried jobs.

Computer consultants, companies involved in hardware and software production, and Internet website developers are among those most active in hiring computer science academics. With demand exceeding the supply, top-ranked computer grads generally receive multiple job offers.

Even students with less impressive academic records are finding that having some knowledge of computers is a distinct advantage in interviewing for a desirable job, especially one that stresses communication capabilities. "When hiring new grads, we look for good analytical, communication, and problem-solving skills," says Al Jones, manager of college recruiting for American Management Systems. Although his company each year employs hundreds of students with nontechnical backgrounds, Jones prefers those with a demonstrated aptitude and interest in information technology. He has noted with satisfaction that most of the liberal arts seniors he interviews are graduating with "pretty sophisticated computer skills."

OPPORTUNITY AND RESPONSIBILITY

If you choose to pursue a career in broadcasting, keep in mind the importance of what you're undertaking and approach the task with respect and enthusiasm. You will be joining a profession with great social, cultural, and commercial responsibilities. Don't apply for admission unless you intend to become a truthful and trustworthy communicator.

Whether you are self-employed or working for a public or private organization, competitive pressures will dictate that you be well equipped—mentally, physically, and emotionally—and stay focused on the right kind of career objectives. Success and contentment won't come primarily from the money you make or the title of your position, but from providing a service that is helpful to others and satisfying to you.

Regardless of where you work or the kind of job you hold, you should be capable of using computers, word processors, fax machines, recording and editing equipment, and other time- and labor-saving machines. Most employers are increasing their use of digital devices, while trimming payrolls and placing heavier responsibilities on fewer people. So it's advisable in job hunting to be multitalented and technically proficient. A small video production firm may have one dexterous employee who doubles as scriptwriter, announcer, and producer. A radio announcer also may be assigned news, music, and engineering duties.

While technical skills and adroitness will improve your chances of finding a good job, holding on to one and getting promoted demand ingenuity and resourcefulness. Brad Dick, editor of *Broadcast Engineering,* says, "The industry will pay and pay well for people who know how to implement tomorrow's technology to help their stations make money. If you're one of them, your future is bright."

Most jobs in TV, radio, cable, and related media require a college degree, or at least some higher education, together with a working knowledge of digital technology, communication skills, a high degree of motivation, and proven ability to work at a fast pace and meet deadlines. You should try to become so reliable and efficient that you will be able to make a comfortable living under ever-changing—even adverse—conditions.

CHAPTER 2

OVERVIEW OF ELECTRONIC COMMUNICATION

Turn on your TV set and right before your eyes, satellite delivery systems give you a front-row seat and a close-up view of people making news not only all over the globe, but even in the outer reaches of space.

Flip a switch on a computer and you have access to vast amounts of information, entertainment, and services. At work, in your car, wherever you go, technology has transformed yesterday's limited world of knowledge and awareness into an unlimited universe of sights, sounds, and impressions.

It is not surprising why so many young people are attracted to broadcasting. They envision a unique opportunity to work in an exciting, ever-changing environment and to engage in humanity's oldest, and arguably most important, civilized activity—the art of communication.

We are now able to communicate so fast that immediacy has become an important consideration in virtually everything we do. Businesses put a premium on speed. Timetables for observation, deliberation, and decision making have been shortened. We are expected to react and respond quickly to every situation. Governments confer in a rapid-fire, informal manner that years ago would have been considered unthinkable. Sometimes diplomats even use television newscasts to communicate and rely on reporters as couriers.

Modern methods of communication strongly influence our lifestyles, our thinking, and our values. We depend on electronic media for information, enlightenment, advertising, and entertainment. They answer our need for companionship, counseling, spiritual support, and baby-sitting. But the arteries of communication are multiplying and changing as merging technologies give birth to countless new websites, cable channels, networks, and various kinds of interactive facilities.

Although these new avenues of communication may cause some loss of jobs in traditional media, they should produce a sizable number of fresh employment opportunities in an expanding multimedia marketplace.

THE BIRTH OF BROADCASTING

As early as the 1860s, while Abraham Lincoln was president, a physicist in Scotland, James Clerk Maxwell, was spending long hours in his laboratory trying to determine for sure that radio waves existed and could be used for communication. Finally, in 1888, another physicist in Germany, Heinrich Rudolph Hertz, confirmed that rapid variations of electric current could be projected into space in the form of radio waves, similar to those of light and heat.

By the 1890s, wireless experiments were being carried out in France, Russia, Italy, Germany, England, and America. Most people considered the tests to be nothing more than a fascinating novelty. But a growing cadre of scientists, military strategists, and business leaders were intrigued by what they heard and supported further research and development.

In 1895, an Italian engineer, Guglielmo Marconi, capitalized on the accumulated findings by successfully sending and receiving radio signals for a short distance. A year later he obtained a British patent for his transmitting device. As the twentieth century dawned, he initiated trans-Atlantic radio tests. Today Marconi is often referred to as the "father of broadcasting."

At the St. Louis World's Fair in 1904, one of the main attractions was a wireless tower operated by a young scientist named Lee DeForest. Three years afterward, he formed a radio telephone company and undertook a prolonged series of experiments designed to convince the public that music and voices could be effectively conveyed by radio telephone.

On January 13, 1910, Enrico Caruso broadcast several songs from the stage of the Metropolitan Opera House in New York. The transmitting antenna was suspended from two fishing poles on the opera house roof. Small groups of radio buffs in New York and New Jersey passed around earphones and listened to the history-making concert.

In 1912, the U.S. Navy adopted the name *Radiotelegraph* for its wireless operations. Later, it originated the term *broadcast* for referring to dissemination of orders to the fleet. By 1915 the Bell Telephone Company was broadcasting frequent voice tests from Arlington, Virginia, and getting reception reports from all over the United States and several foreign countries.

RADIO GROWTH AND REGULATION

America's first radio licensing law was enacted in 1912. Although it was an inadequate answer to the needs of this rapidly growing medium, the legislation served for fifteen years as the country's basic rules for radio operations. The law authorized assignment of wavelengths and operational times to applicants. Different spectrum positions were allotted to ships, governmental agencies, and amateurs. Provision was made for some experimental permits. Soon after the law went into effect, more than a thousand broadcasters, including many colleges and universities, applied for and received licenses. Hundreds of additional licenses were issued in the years that followed.

Initially, all broadcasting was noncommercial. In 1919, some "radiotelephone experimenters" received permission to operate on a "limited" commercial basis.

Following the first National Radio Conference in 1922, a new type of AM transmitter was authorized for use, and maximum power usage was increased to 1,000 watts. Demand for licenses remained so strong that the standard broadcast band was broadened from 550 to 1,500 kilocycles, and transmitter power was upped again to 5,000 watts.

As the number of AM radio stations multiplied, the air became cluttered with signals, causing serious interference problems. The situation went uncorrected because existing laws lacked enforcement provisions. Many broadcasters were illegally changing frequencies, boosting power, and transmitting longer hours than authorized. At the 1925 Fourth National Radio Conference, concerned delegates appealed to the government to make radio stations play by the rules.

The Dill-White Radio Act of 1927 created a five-member Federal Radio Commission and empowered its members to issue licenses, allocate frequencies, and control wattage of transmitters. The act designated the secretary of commerce to inspect radio stations, examine their methods of operation, and assign permanent call letters only to qualified licensees. It was a start in the right direction, but a more comprehensive law was still needed. One was finally passed seven years later.

THE COMMUNICATIONS ACT OF 1934

In 1933, President Franklin D. Roosevelt requested the secretary of commerce to appoint an interdepartmental committee to study the nation's electronic communications needs and problems. The committee recommended that Congress establish a single agency to regulate all interstate and foreign communication by wire and radio, including telephone, telegraph, and broadcast. As a result, The Communications Act of 1934 was passed. It incorporated some provisions from the earlier Radio Act, but it added much-needed regulation and supervision measures and created a seven-member Federal Communications Commission to administer the unified legislation. This is the statute under which the FCC has operated since July 11, 1934; however, the size of the commission was reduced in 1983 to five members.

These are some of the ways the FCC regulates broadcasting:

1. It allocates space in the radio frequency spectrum to all broadcast services and to many auxiliary and nonbroadcast services that employ radio technology.
2. It assigns location, frequency, and power to stations in each service within the allocated frequency bands.
3. It regulates broadcasting by inspection of existing stations to ensure that they operate in accordance with FCC rules and technical provisions. Serious violations are subject to monetary fines and even revocation of license.
4. The commission also assigns call letters, issues transmitter and operational licenses, processes requests for transfer of license ownership, and, at renewal time, reviews each station's record to see if it is operating in the public interest.

AM BROADCASTING

AM—the oldest system of broadcasting—is sometimes referred to as Standard Broadcast. It is designed to convert sounds collected by a microphone into electrical impulses, or audio waves, of varying intensity. These audio waves are amplified and impressed on "carrier" waves that modulate in amplitude to correspond to the strength and frequency of the audio waves they are carrying or transmitting. Thus, the name *A*mplitude *M*odulation, or AM broadcast.

The FCC has created these AM broadcast channels:

Clear channel—Stations in this category serve wide areas and are protected from objectionable interference within their primary service areas, and in some instances, secondary areas.

Regional channel—This channel is for class B and class D stations that operate to serve primarily a principal population center and the contiguous rural area.

Local channel—Local channel stations operate unlimited time and serve primarily a community and the immediately contiguous suburban and rural areas.

Every AM station is assigned an FCC classification.

Class A stations operate on a clear channel with power of no less than 10,000 watts nor more than 50,000 watts. They have no time restrictions and are designed to provide primary and secondary service to a widespread area. A limited number of clear channel stations have nondirectional 50 kilowatt transmitters that send out an "umbrella" pattern of sky wave and ground wave signals to local and distant listeners.

Class B stations are designed to render service only over a primary area. They may operate unlimited time with minimum power of 250 watts and maximum of 50 kilowatts. (Class B stations in the 1605–1705 kilohertz band are limited to 10-kilowatt power.)

Class C stations operate on a local channel and are designed to render service only over a primary area that may be reduced if found to cause interference with other stations. Power ranges from 250 to 1,000 watts. Though no lesser-powered stations are being licensed, some 100 watters still exist.

Class D stations operate either daytime, limited time, or unlimited time with nighttime power less than 250 watts. Daytime power ranges from 250 watts to 50,000 watts.

FM RADIO

A few scientists knew about frequency modulation (FM), when broadcasting was in its infancy, but the general public didn't find out until the 1930s, after a technical wizard named Edwin H. Armstrong began publicizing the superior qualities of FM. Finally, in 1940, the FCC got around to allocating thirty-five channels for commercial FM and five for noncommercial, educational FM.

On October 31, 1940, the commission granted construction permits for the first fifteen FM stations. By the time World War II halted all such activity, thirty FM outlets were on the air, reaching about 400,000 homes. Growth of FM remained slow for several decades until the public gradually found out that FM offered high fidelity, clarity, and less static than AM. Today it is far more popular than AM radio.

In 1962, the FCC divided the country into three FM zones and created three classes of commercial FM stations:

Class A stations, assigned to all zones, are allowed a maximum of 3 kilowatts effective radiated power and maximum antenna height of 300 feet.

Class B stations, assigned to zone I and IA, are allowed a maximum power of 50,000 watts and maximum antenna height of 500 feet.

Class C stations, assigned to zone II, are allowed up to 100 kilowatts of power and maximum antenna height of 2,000 feet.

In addition to their regular programming, FM stations can apply for a Subsidiary Communications Authorization to multiplex a variety of nonbroadcast subscription services such as in-store music or special kinds of information.

STEREO BROADCASTING

Stereophonic broadcasting was authorized by the FCC in 1961, and since then most FM stations, and some AM, transmit all of their programs in stereo. Many television stations and cable channels also provide service in stereo to their audiences.

DEVELOPMENT OF TELEVISION

The history of television closely parallels that of radio because growth of the wireless movement intensified interest in transmitting sight as well as sound. As early as 1884, a German scientist, Paul Nipkow, developed a scanning device for sending pictures by wireless. Three years later, another German, K. F. Braun, invented the cathode ray tube. In 1907, A. A. Campbell-Swinton in England, and Boris Rosing in Russia, working independently, almost simultaneously worked out the basic principles of modern television. Four years later, Swinton designed a television camera.

All of these pioneering efforts coalesced in the United States when V. K. Zworykin, an immigrant from Russia, applied in 1923 for a patent on the iconoscope camera tube. Modern orthicon and image-orthicon cameras are descendants of Zworykin's brainchild.

By 1927, several American broadcasting stations were experimenting with television. One program, transmitted by wire from Washington to New York, featured Herbert Hoover, who was then secretary of commerce. RCA demonstrated large-screen TV in 1930 from the stage of a Manhattan theater. In 1936, the British Broadcasting Corporation introduced a public television service using all electronic equipment. Soon afterward, seventeen experimental TV stations were operating in this country.

Franklin Roosevelt became the first president to be televised when he opened the New York World's Fair in 1939. That same year saw the first telecast of major league baseball, college football, and professional boxing.

After World War II, television began to expand nationwide and become a major new entertainment and advertising medium. Millions of TV sets, camcorders, VCRs, and video programs are now manufactured and sold annually. Thousands of people are engaged in what has evolved into a vast, diversified, and ever-changing television industry.

THE TELECOMMUNICATIONS ACT OF 1996

Passage of the Telecommunications Act of 1996 was hailed by many advocates for change as a landmark media bill that would create a multitude of jobs, encourage diversity of voices and viewpoints, and usher in a new information age. Only time will determine the accuracy of that highly optimistic opinion. But the law has triggered a flurry of buyouts and corporate mergers. It also has intensified rivalry among phone companies, cable system operators, and other local and long-distance communication systems.

The law removes all restrictions on the number of AM and FM radio stations that one company can have, but limits ownership in individual markets as follows: a maximum of eight radio properties in markets with more than 45 stations; up to seven in markets with 30 to 44 stations; as many as six in markets with 15 to 29 stations; and a maximum of five in markets with less than 15 stations.

Rules regarding television also have been relaxed to permit a company to own an unlimited number of TV stations nationwide, provided their combined reach does not exceed 35 percent of the country's television audience. However, the rule limiting ownership to one TV station per market remains unchanged.

Other provisions of the Telecommunications Act include the following:

1. Permits common ownership of cable systems and broadcast networks.
2. Extends the license terms of TV and radio stations to eight years.
3. Immediately ends rate regulation of smaller cable systems and provides for eventual rate deregulation of larger systems.
4. Allows TV networks to start and own an additional broadcast network.

5. Requires new TV sets to come equipped with a V-chip for screening out objectionable programming.
6. Imposes fines for transmission of pornography on the Internet.

COMMERCIAL BROADCASTING IN THE UNITED STATES

Most broadcasting stations and cable systems in the United States are commercial operations engaged in selling programs and spot announcements to advertisers. Educational and noncommercial facilities—principally owned and managed by educational and religious institutions—do not sell advertising time but are allowed to solicit limited amounts of financial support from advertisers and to briefly identify a donor's products and services.

The Federal Communications Commission ordinarily does not prescribe the content or amount of subject matter to be broadcast. Each licensee is expected to continually ascertain the needs and interests of the people in its coverage area and to respond with appropriate programming. However, the FCC does require television stations to air at least three hours of shows each week for children.

Since 1965, the public has been permitted to inspect certain records maintained by broadcast stations. These include licenses, ownership documents, network and syndication contracts, and employment reports. This information may be used by individuals who wish to either complain about the way a station is being operated or challenge continuance of its license, which must be renewed every eight years.

Although the FCC is forbidden by law from exercising broadcast censorship, it can prohibit transmission of false, obscene, or fraudulent information. Penalties for violations range from reprimands and cease-and-desist orders to fines of up to $25,000. If an offense is extremely serious, the FCC can revoke a license or deny its renewal.

There are two ways to obtain a broadcast license: by applying for an unused frequency or channel, or by purchasing a station already in existence. The latter course is generally preferred because it is quicker and less complicated. In fact, the buying and selling of broadcast properties has become a huge and very active business.

ELECTRONIC MEDIA CONVERGENCE

As broadcasting and other electronic media adopt digital-age technology and become more competitive, the twenty-first century may someday be remembered as the time when conventional methods of transmitting and receiving sights and sounds reinvented themselves and metamorphosed into more flexible and versatile forms of communication.

That prediction comes from Dr. Jennings Bryant, professor of telecommunications at the University of Alabama, who notes that since the Telecommunications Act of 1996 permits media to compete in certain areas from which they were formerly restricted, we are seeing many corporate mergers, acquisitions, and the development of hybrid digital devices that combine communication functions.

Bryant envisions computers, radio, television, and cable eventually sharing and utilizing many of the same audio, video, and interactive capabilities. Companies are already manufacturing a "set-top box" that is designed to sit atop a television set and provide quick and easy access to the worldwide web. This combining of television and computer functions is evident in another way. Manufacturers are now producing computers that can double as television sets, as well as software that enables viewers to watch TV on their computer monitors.

Adding to this complicated picture, cable interests, telephone companies, satellite delivery systems, print media, and broadcasters are all participating in this massive intermingling of information gathering, packaging, and distribution technology.

"It's almost impossible to judge who will be the winners and losers," says Bryant. Ultimately, from out of the competition, compromise, and convergence will come a new age of interactive broadcasting and narrowcasting and the promise of many new career opportunities in electronic communication.

YOU AND DIGITAL TECHNOLOGY

The United States is steadily evolving into a computerized communication society. More than half of the American workforce is engaged in the production and transmission of digital information. This vast army accounts for two-thirds of the nation's working hours and labor costs. Similar conditions exist in Canada, Germany, Japan, and other hi-tech countries.

Digital systems for acquiring, storing, and delivering data are multiplying by the millions, radically altering the way organizations and individuals share ideas, run their businesses, and lead their lives.

This revolution in digital technology has profoundly affected all forms of broadcasting. Radio, television, and cable are heavily involved in the creation and transmission of digital-processed information and entertainment, much of it personalized and interactive. Their operations and countless others that maintain websites on the Internet have opened up numerous new jobs.

If you seek employment in this rapidly evolving industry, you will have many options. But to qualify for them you will have to be well educated, both academically and technically. Most broadcasting employees now are required to be skillful and versatile professionals who are capable of working dependably in more than one area of responsibility.

Should you decide to become a twenty-first-century broadcaster, be prepared to study and utilize the latest and most efficient communication technology. Keep in mind that you are learning to be a multimedia expert who is technically, culturally, and socially proficient in responding to the needs and preferences of a discriminating, interactive public. If you apply yourself to this task with adequate knowledge and the right attitude, you will likely find success on the digital supersky way.

CHAPTER 3

BROADCASTING AND NARROWCASTING IN THE UNITED STATES AND CANADA

Residents of the United States and Canada are better informed than anyone else in the world, thanks to an avalanche of news and knowledge that flows into our homes and offices, night and day, from a multitude of broadcasting and narrowcasting sources. We live in an electronic media society that magnifies our awareness and motivates us to get involved, actually or vicariously, in what is happening locally and elsewhere.

Even in remote areas, viewers and listeners are privy to, and participants in, a constant and rapid exchange of ideas and information. We are fast approaching the time when virtually everyone will possess technology for conversing aurally and visually with other individuals throughout the world.

"We are all going through a time of great change," says NBC news anchor Tom Brokaw. "I did not believe at this stage of my career that there would be so many new opportunities, with cyber-technology and interactive possibilities—all the new channels that are being created—the enormous appetite that exists for information and communication, and the willingness of big companies to try and meet the demand. I find it exciting and I think we are all privileged to work in the field that we do."

Thousands of professional broadcasters are happily employed in today's hi-tech, mass-media environment. An even larger number of narrowcasters work for communication companies that cater to the needs and interests of smaller groups.

These different types of video and audio technology normally compete for advertising and public support, but many are now cooperating—combining resources and techniques to improve services and create new forms of communication. One such example is a multimedia device that functions as a computer, TV set, telephone, VCR, and video-game machine.

High-speed, broad and narrowband methods of communication in the United States and Canada comprise what is commonly referred to as the information superhighway. It includes radio, TV, cable, telephone, computer, satellite, and all other terrestrial and wireless technology used for public and private communication.

THE BROADCASTING JOB MARKET

Employment opportunities for broadcasters are expected to increase during the next decade as new forms of electronic media combine the capabilities of radio, television, cable, and computer. Numerous jobs are now available for professional broadcasters with knowledge of digital technology. (See Tables 3.1, 3.2, and 3.4.)

Websites and cyberspace networks are hiring former radio and television technicians, programmers, graphic artists, account executives, sales managers, financial reporters, marketing directors, meteorologists, news reporters, writers, and editors.

Thousands of men and women, trained as broadcasters, are finding jobs with public and private organizations, where they work as advertising, sales, marketing, and promotion managers; public relations and public information officers; and directors of development. One of the best job markets for electronic communicators exists in the retail business community, where many firms do intensive radio and TV advertising, marketing, and sales promotion. Applicants for these positions should have strong written, verbal, and technical skills.

Armed with a degree in broadcasting and some professional experience, particularly with computers and digital communication devices, you should be able to find a good job with one or more of the following: business corporations, major publications, on-line editions of newspapers, national and regional cable networks, professional associations and societies, museums, libraries, syndicated news services, advertising agencies, video and audio production studios, medical TV facilities, school systems, colleges and universities, government agencies, research firms, religious organizations, TV and radio program syndicators, satellite delivery systems, trade and technical schools, and fund-raising organizations.

As for dreams you may have of someday being a network news anchor or host of your own TV show, don't give up on such ideas. If you are exceptionally talented and determined to succeed, you may some day be as well known and popular as Oprah Winfrey, Larry King, or Jay Leno.

TELEVISION IN AMERICA

Television plays many roles in the lives of the American people. Research indicates that a heavy percentage of viewers look to TV every day to: provide news and information—90 percent; provide entertainment—81 percent; give leaders a communication link with the public—76 percent; educate—68 percent; bring the nation together—58 percent; serve as a break from real life—55 percent; help shape American culture—55 percent; help consumers make purchasing decisions—48 percent; teach character and values to children and teenagers—48 percent.

Congress and the Federal Communications Commission have authorized some 2,000 television channels to operate in communities throughout the United States. The country is divided into three geographical zones, each of which is permitted a certain number of VHF (very high frequency) and UHF (ultra high frequency) channels. The channel number and zone of a station determine its maximum power, antenna height, and the distance it must be separated from other stations on the same channel.

Commercial TV stations are required to broadcast at least twenty-eight hours a week. Most stay on the air longer than that. Many operate twenty-four hours a day, seven days a week. Some TV outlets use low-power translators and boosters to carry their signal into hard-to-reach areas. TV stations also reach additional viewers by way of cable systems and computer websites.

A majority of television stations are affiliated with major networks such as ABC, CBS, NBC, and Fox. An affiliate usually carries at least three hours of network programs at night and some daytime shows. Stations obtain additional programs from networks and syndication companies that specialize in the sale and distribution of news, weather, sports, music, comedy, movies, cultural programs, and special events.

The FCC is requiring that all TV stations, by the year 2006, switch from analog to digital broadcasting systems. The purpose is to provide American viewers with higher quality video-audio service.

TV Independents

A television station that is not affiliated with a network is commonly referred to as an independent. Instead of relying on a network to supply much of its news and programming, the independent outlet develops many of its own productions and purchases or leases programs from outside sources.

Independents customarily rely heavily on using motion pictures and reruns of shows previously shown on network-affiliated stations. Some independents narrowcast by specializing in one type of video, such as religion,

Opportunities in Broadcasting Careers

Table 3.1   U.S. Radio/Television Employment

Job Category	Total	Female	Male	Minority
Officials/Managers	29,572	10,463	19,109	4,145
Professionals	48,939	17,236	31,703	9,206
Technicians	25,417	3,781	21,636	6,050
Sales Workers	22,690	12,096	10,594	3,180
Office/Clerical	18,050	15,929	2,121	5,807
Craftspeople	696	108	588	224
Operatives	622	88	534	221
Laborers	178	20	158	97
Services	452	87	365	281
TOTAL	146,616	59,808	86,808	29,211

Source: Equal Employment Opportunity Trend Report, prepared for the FCC Industry EEO Unit, July 4, 1997.

news, sports, or talk. KTVU, a California independent, operates one of the highest-rated news departments in the San Francisco area.

Since it produces and markets many of its own programs, a well-run independent station can be a busy and stimulating place to work. Opportunities to handle various kinds of assignments give employees of independent stations more well-rounded experience than they might obtain at a network affiliate.

Television and Cable Networks

Networks are almost as old as broadcasting. They originated during the pioneering days of radio and brought distant voices and events into the nation's living rooms. TV networks came into existence shortly after World War II, relaying their first programs by phone lines or mail. They now feed affiliated stations by satellite, microwave, or coax-cable.

Before cable TV blanketed the country, most viewers in the United States could only watch the network offerings aired by local VHF and UHF stations. Now cable and satellite systems have vastly increased the available choices. More than two-hundred cable networks narrowcast various types of specialized programming, and the average cable system makes room for forty or fifty of them. CNN, CNBC, New England Cable, and numerous other networks deal only with news. Other networks concentrate solely on religion, comedy, animals, sports, public affairs (C-Span), home shopping, or some other specialty. Several networks transmit only Spanish-language programs.

RADIO RESURGENCE

Despite widespread predictions that new electronic media will eventually replace traditional forms of broadcasting, radio remains healthy and individual stations are selling at high prices. Since the FCC deregulated the industry, aggressive radio groups have been acquiring scores of FM and AM properties. Some companies own a hundred or more and as many as eight in a single market. By 1998 more than a fourth of all radio stations in the United States were in the hands of a few giant conglomerates. Opinions differ about the merits of this trend.

Multiple station owners are able to cut expenses and make more profit by eliminating overlapping staff members; using syndicated music, talk, and news services; and relying heavily on automated equipment. This has reduced the number of jobs available at individual stations, but consolidation of ownership is creating new opportunities for professionals who are qualified to handle multistation responsibilities in management, programming, sales, marketing, engineering, and promotion. For example, retail specialists are being hired to develop and sell programming suitable for airing on a group of commonly owned stations—features such as outdoor music concerts, athletic events, and conventions.

Broadcast Consultant Tom Barnes foresees this trend continuing, with teams of experts working together for a group of stations. Radio programming and selling concepts, in his opinion, will undergo group development, review, revision, standardization, and sale. This leaves little room for recognition of individuals. The emphasis is on anonymous collaboration. When successful, members of the team are rewarded with high salaries and bonuses.

The twenty-first century will no doubt see further changes in how radio is bought, sold, and utilized. Many different formats and specialized radio services are sure to be tried in years to come. Some will fail, while others become popular and profitable. Group ownership may decline and single stations increase in answer to public demand for more localized diversity in programming. All of this activity should generate numerous exciting career opportunities for radio broadcasters.

Audio Personalities

Every radio station, FM or AM, radiates a distinctive sound and personality. A great many factors are involved in creating and maintaining this image at a high level of popularity to entice listeners and attract advertisers. Foremost in determining a station's personality is its programming. Thousands of stations depend primarily on the kind of music they play to define who they are. But competition among stations that use similar music formats sometimes makes it difficult to distinguish one from the other. (See Table 3.3.)

Some stations are known and preferred primarily because of talented performers heard on daily shows. If a station plays little or no music, or virtually all music and no talk, its personality may largely reflect its size and power, the philosophy of its management, its marketing methods, how it is advertised and promoted, or the importance that the public places on the service it delivers.

Job requirements vary at radio stations, depending on the nature of their programming; the sound-image that the facility is attempting to project; and the demographic segment of the population it is trying to reach and please. Working as a disc jockey on a youth-oriented station is quite different from being a newscaster or talk-show host on an outlet that appeals to adults twenty-five and older.

There is an obvious need for poorly defined radio stations to work harder at building a positive sound personality. Providing this kind of leadership can open the door to a rewarding radio career.

Growth of Radio Networks

For many years four major radio networks—ABC, NBC, CBS and Mutual—were dominant in America, each providing hundreds of affiliated stations with a variety of programs. But the coming of television caused radio networks to lose listeners and affiliates. They appeared doomed to extinction.

Interest in radio networks revived, however, when they stopped variety programming and started creating audio services of the type now commonly heard. As a result, thousands of radio stations are presently affiliated with

Table 3.2 Size of Broadcast Staffs (U.S. Television/Radio Stations)

	Average (All Stations)	Small Market	Median	Large Market
Full-Time TV Jobs	65	29	50	116
Part-Time TV Jobs	12	7	12	17
Full-Time Radio Jobs	25	16	20	40
Part-Time Radio Jobs	5	4	4	8

Source: 1997 estimates based on annual surveys conducted by the National Association of Broadcasters and the Broadcast Financial Management Association, and personal research by the author.

Table 3.3 Top Radio Formats in the United States

	Primary Format	Total	Commercial	Non-Comm.	% AM	% FM
1	Country	2,505	2,491	14	35%	65%
2	News, Talk	1,567	1,111	456	68%	32%
3	Adult Contemporary	917	902	15	25%	75%
4	Oldies	760	755	5	39%	61%
5	Religion (Teaching, Variety)	739	404	335	49%	51%
6	Adult Standards	558	551	7	85%	15%
7	Spanish	516	474	42	59%	41%
8	Variety	426	50	376	13%	87%
9	Top-40 (CHR)	401	358	43	3%	97%
10	Contemporary Christian	389	159	230	17%	83%
11	Alternative Rock	366	94	272	2%	98%
12	Soft Adult Contemporary	349	346	3	21%	79%
13	Southern Gospel	285	255	30	71%	29%
14	Rock	272	262	10	6%	94%
15	Adult Hits, Hot AC	262	260	2	5%	95%
16	Classic Rock	242	240	2	4%	96%
17	Sports	220	220		96%	4%
18	Black Gospel	218	208	10	85%	15%
19	Urban, R&B	196	169	27	23%	77%
20	Classic Hits	173	172	1	2%	98%
21	Classical, Fine Arts	161	44	117	4%	96%
22	Jazz	161	92	69	7%	93%
23	New Rock, Modern Rock	137	137		3%	97%
24	Urban AC	134	134		29%	71%
25	Ethnic	82	75	7	74%	26%
26	Modern AC	70	70		1%	99%
27	Gospel	60	37	23	57%	43%
28	Easy Listening	57	49	8	23%	77%
29	R&B Oldies	46	46		72%	28%
30	Pre-Teen	40	40		98%	3%
	Not available or changing	4	2	2	0%	100%
	Total operating stations	12,313	10,207	2,106	39%	61%

Source: M Street Corp., P.O. Box 1479, Madison, Tennessee 37116-1479, November 1997.

one or more networks. Many of them depend on networks to supply most or all of their daily programming.

About 20 national radio networks now produce various kinds of music, talk, and news. More than 100 regional networks, and several hundred news services and programming companies, also provide for the needs of broadcasters.

Thousands of radio stations aim their programming at specific demographic groups. As they strive to reach and sell to people of a particular race, age, and social and economic level, radio networks and syndicators cooperate by supplying appropriate programming.

It costs less to purchase or contract for this kind of audio service than to produce it with local staff talent. Therefore, networks are likely to remain popular with broadcasters. This, in turn, should mean a sizable number of jobs for persons qualified to develop and market network and syndicated productions.

The Hometown Station

Despite the prevalence of automated radio stations that feature only music, talk, or news, a sizable number of stations continue to do live, comprehensive programming, melding various information and entertainment elements into their daily schedule. Such stations usually subscribe to a radio news service and may affiliate with a national or regional network to fill some programming needs. But by and large, a traditional "hometown station" concentrates on being a loyal and dependable voice of the community. It is an excellent training ground for beginners in broadcasting.

U.S. CABLE TV

For many years the American people chose their favorite television shows by dialing to specific stations. Millions still do, but vast numbers of viewers now make their selections by switching to various cable channels. By 1998 there were almost 12,000 cable systems serving 65 million subscribers in 34,000 communities. The average cable household paid $20 a month for access to fifty channels. Some cable systems offer a hundred or more channels.

Based on the alternative concept of narrowcasting, more than 100 national companies specialize in supplying movies and other programs to cable systems on such subjects as news, weather, sports, travel, animals, medicine, financial reports, education, public affairs, comedy, and home shopping. Foreign language programming is plentiful and growing in markets with large ethnic audiences. Cable employment grew from 5,000 in 1978 to 116,000 in 1997. Total cable advertising revenues for 1997 exceeded $7 billion.

Table 3.4 U.S. Cable Television Employment

Job Category	Total	Female	Male	Minority
Officials/Managers	17,046	6,117	10,929	2,645
Professionals	5,338	2,554	2,784	900
Technicians	17,351	1,400	15,951	3,899
Sales Workers	10,594	4,680	5,914	3,004
Office/Clerical	40,478	34,071	6,407	14,791
Craftspeople	11,843	454	11,389	2,894
Operatives	16,585	824	15,761	5,378
Laborers	1,030	124	906	329
Services	266	83	183	91
Total	120,531	50,307	70,224	33,931

Source: Equal Employment Opportunity Trend Report, prepared for the FCC Industry EEO Unit, July 4, 1997.

Cable TV now blankets 98 percent of the country, and eventually the entire nation will be cable-connected. Although not a broadcast service in the strictest sense, cable TV is regulated by the FCC, which requires systems serving more than 3,500 subscribers to do a certain amount of local programming. About 5,000 systems maintain studios and average producing twenty-three hours of weekly programs. Some 3,000 systems sell locally originated advertising at rates from $2 to $600 per thirty-second spot.

More than 200 satellite-fed networks provide programming for cable systems. Several of the most popular are devoted to news and public affairs. There are also a dozen regional cable news networks and two dozen regional sports networks. Cable News Network (CNN) transmits by satellite twenty-four hours a day to viewers in the United States, Canada, and more than 100 other countries.

Cable systems maintain one or more public access channels where local groups and individuals create and produce their own entertainment and informational programs. Some systems sell classified ads and market language courses, educational classes, and video shopping services.

As innovations in digital and fiber optic technology transform the broadcasting industry, cable companies are benefiting from their ability to provide new channels, sharper pictures, and movies on demand, plus a number of broadband interactive services that compete with telecommunications companies, direct broadcast satellite, and Internet providers. These include audio, video, and data phone services as well as high-speed modem service.

Tiny Broadcasters

Some broadcasting facilities serve small, selective audiences and provide interesting, even unique, services. In 1996, Bob Montgomery and Gary Cox bought several secondhand cameras, built a basement studio, and started their own little television station, MATV, in Dobson, North Carolina. Together they produce twenty hours of local programming a week, featuring talented hometown performers. They also handle all of the administrative duties, operate and repair the equipment, and sell advertising time. The station has no transmitter. Instead it reaches 20,000 homes via two cable companies in the area.

John Ford, head of the Vancouver Aquarium, runs an even smaller "all-whale" radio station. The only performers heard on the FM outlet are killer whales, whose singing and conversing are captured by underwater hydrophones. These unusual sounds provide research material for Ford and fascinating listening for a sizable audience of whale lovers. The nonprofit station has received favorable recognition as a valuable educational and entertainment medium. Numerous other examples of miniature broadcasting ventures can be found in the United States. Few make much money, but they can make satisfying career choices for individuals with atypical interests.

Related Technologies

Pay Cable. This offers subscribers channels of special programming for which they pay a certain amount above the basic monthly charges. Home Box Office Inc. initiated the first national interconnected pay network in 1975. In addition to contracting for program services of this type, many cable systems also lease channels to pay-program operators or manage their own pay cable service and obtain programming from outside sources.

Pay-Per-View (PPV). This is a method used by cable systems to market performances and events that would otherwise be seen only by the audience at the scene. Just as in-house cable systems in hotels offer feature films for a set fee, pay-per-view events are limited to spectators who pay for the privilege. To prevent people from watching without paying, programs are transmitted in scrambled signals that can be deciphered only by sets equipped with decoders.

Viewer Controlled TV (VCTV). A new form of pay-per-view now being tested makes available to customers an entire library of feature films, any one of which can be selected for viewing by pushing a button on a home selector. This promises to become a major success in video marketing.

Low-Power Television (LPTV). Essentially television translator stations, these low-powered installations rebroadcast the signals of full-service stations and are used primarily to serve areas where normal TV reception is inadequate.

Multipoint Distribution Service (MDS). This system uses microwave to transmit video, data, text, or other services to customer-selected locations within a metropolitan area. Operators generally lease most of their time to pay-movie entrepreneurs who provide programming to hotels, apartment buildings, and homes.

Satellite Master Antenna Systems (SMATV). Similar to cable systems, SMATV is not federally regulated and operates in limited areas. An earth station aimed at a cable satellite receives and transmits programming to individual apartment buildings, condominiums, or private housing developments.

High-Definition Television (HDTV). This method of video production, transmission, and display offers viewers a superior kind of video and audio service. Color, sharpness of image, and fidelity of sound are all enhanced by this Japanese-developed technology. Some form of HDTV is expected to set the standard for television in the future.

Wireless Cable

Wireless cable transmits over microwave frequencies, and most systems provide twenty or more network channels to their customers. These channels are supplied through the combined facilities of MDS—multipoint distribution service, MMDS—multichannel multipoint distribution service, ITFS—instructional television fixed service, and OFS—operational fixed service. In all, thirty-three channels are available, twenty of which come from ITFS and require transmitting five hours of educational programming per channel each week. Wireless cable is now in thirty countries, with the heaviest concentration in Eastern Europe and Latin America. Early systems in New York, Detroit, Washington, and Cleveland were not successful, but the Wireless Cable Association, 1140 Connecticut Avenue, NW, Suite 810, Washington, DC 20036, is optimistic about future growth, especially the potential of pay-per-view wireless.

DBS

This video service bypasses networks, cable systems, and individual TV stations by transmitting from satellites stationed 22,300 miles above the earth to decoding disk antennas of individual subscribers. It only took four years for digital broadcast satellite systems to sign-up six million customers. The business continues to grow as additional households contract for DBS delivery of 175 or more channels of TV fare.

Some home satellite sets are equipped to receive even local TV stations, thereby eliminating the need to subscribe to a cable company for this service. D-VHS machines also are available for making recordings of satellite-delivered programs. Satellite companies are listed annually in the *Broadcasting & Cable Yearbook,* along with information about networks, common carriers, and program syndicators who use satellites to serve TV, radio, and cable operations. The federal government, phone companies, and international business firms are all big users of satellites.

INTERACTIVE NARROWCASTING

Digital technology, satellites, fiber optics, and video compression have made possible new forms of tightly focused communication called narrowcasting. Devices now on the market enable individuals or small groups of people to converse aurally and visually, transact business, and receive or exchange e-mail, data, information, and entertainment. It is even easy to set up interactive networks where everyone on-line is welcome to participate. Because narrowcasting offers so many useful options, it is destined to develop in many forms and create numerous career opportunities.

ISDN

Integrated Services Digital Network (ISDN) is a method of digital communication that allows you to talk, send, and receive data, and transmit video and faxes on a conventional phone line. The digitized transmissions are reassembled at the other end of the line into high-quality imagery and sound. As a result, ISDN is being increasingly used for remote broadcasts and video conferencing. Ann Gartlan, veteran actress/announcer, has her own ISDN studio and voices promotional spots for NBC's *Today* show and other clients.

PUBLIC BROADCASTING

Although broadcasting in America is primarily a commercial system supported by revenues from advertisers, hundreds of noncommercial radio and television stations in the country provide the public with educational and cultural programming.

The government initiated this type of broadcasting by issuing some of the first AM radio licenses to educational institutions. By 1925, more than 170 schools and colleges owned and operated their own stations. The FCC no longer grants permits for AM educational stations, and few remain on the air; but it continues to encourage public broadcasting by allocating FM and TV channels to noncommercial applicants. More than 1,900 noncommercial FMs and 365 noncommercial TV stations are on the air, or under construction. Many are licensed to educational institutions or systems.

Public broadcasting facilities are not required to stay on the air for any specified number of hours, but they are expected to ascertain and respond to educational and cultural needs of the communities they serve. Their daily programs are beamed to millions of students in classrooms and also are available to the general public.

The Corporation for Public Broadcasting, a nongovernmental statutory organization, located at 901 E Street, NW, Washington, DC 20004–2037, was created to provide support and guidance to public radio and television stations. It receives both federal funding and private donations. Some of this money goes directly to individual stations, but most of it is used to subsidize programming for member stations of National Public Radio and Public Broadcasting Service (TV).

National Public Radio, (NPR), 635 Massachusetts Avenue, Washington, DC, 20001, is a noncommercial, satellite-delivered radio system that provides some 540 FM stations with programs and promotional and fund-raising assistance. NPR also represents its member stations in Washington on issues affecting broadcasters.

Public Broadcasting Service, (PBR), 1320 Braddock Place, Alexandria, Virginia 22314–1698, is a nonprofit corporation that supplies programming, research, and promotional assistance to most of the nation's public television stations. The Educational Broadcasting Corp., Owner of WNET, New York, is a major producer of programs for this service. Numerous other TV shows are developed for PBS by regional networks and stations WGBH in Boston and WQRD in Pittsburgh.

Only a limited number of jobs exist at public TV and radio stations. Staffs are small and salaries are modest. But working conditions usually are favorable, and the pace generally is less stressful than in commercial operations. An added incentive is the opportunity to work in a field that is dedicated to education.

Other Public TV–Radio Systems

Public Radio International. PRI, located at 100 North Sixth Street, Suite 900A, Minneapolis, Minnesota 55403, acquires, develops, funds, and distributes radio programs via satellite to 540 public FM stations in the United

States, Guam, and Puerto Rico. In cooperation with National Public Radio and the Corporation for Public Broadcasting, PRI serves all of Europe with twenty-four-hour English-language programming, "America One," transmitted by satellite, cable, and AM and FM radio stations. PRI also cooperates with the British Broadcasting Corp., and WGBH in Boston, to produce a weekly radio news magazine, "The World," aired in Europe and the United States.

Campus Radio Stations. In 1948, the FCC authorized schools to obtain broadcast licenses for 10-watt FM-educational stations. With low-powered equipment, easily installed and simple to operate, this type station transmits a weak signal to a limited campus area.

College Carrier-Current Radio. Some schools and colleges have small radio stations that transmit their programming by carrier current. Reception is confined to on-campus listening. This kind of station does not require FCC registration, but it can provide practical experience for student broadcasters.

Closed-Circuit TV and Radio. Many schools have closed-circuit systems linking classrooms for instructional purposes. This service is transmitted by cable. Since no actual broadcast is involved, such operations are not subject to government regulation.

Satellite Education Resources Consortium. This organization of educators and public broadcasting systems in more than twenty states is a cooperative venture for developing and delivering instructional resources to students and teachers. One such method, interactive television, permits students at home or in a classroom to see and converse with an instructor in a remote studio. A number of state school systems use this methodology to teach courses in math, science, and foreign languages.

LINKNET, Inc. This association of public broadcasting stations stretches from New York to Hawaii. Member stations share and swap information by using satellites, computers, and telephones.

LICENSED LOW-POWER NARROWCASTING

The FCC issues licenses for several types of low-power AM, FM, and TV operations. The limits on power and coverage radius are: AM—250 watts, 25 miles; FM—100 watts, 4 miles; TV—100 watts, 4 miles. Stations may be either commercial or noncommercial but transmit only educational or informational messages. Some air weather reports, travel advisories, and promotional announcements for parks, museums, or tourist attractions. Others serve as mobile relay stations. Still others supply public safety and special emergency radio services, or industrial and land transportation radio services. These low-power outlets narrowcast to a small, specific type of audience.

UNLICENSED LOW-POWER NARROWCASTING

The FCC permits the manufacture and operation of small AM and FM transmitters that generate a maximum effective radiated power of .01 microwatts. They are designed to blanket a coverage radius of only 200 to 300 feet. No license is required, and there are no restrictions on hours of operation. A typical transmitter—weighing only 2.5 pounds—functions automatically with an audiocassette or digital chip mechanism. Schools and churches use such facilities to communicate with their respective audiences. Banks, real estate firms, and drive-in restaurants rely on these miniature transmitters for sales and marketing purposes. Some residential neighborhoods operate their own low power radio bulletin board. FCC rules do not permit unlicensed stations of this kind to be heard on television broadcast bands.

ELECTRONIC MEDIA IN CANADA

Quite a few famous broadcasters have launched their careers in our neighbor nation, Canada, and it continues to be an active training ground and job market. Peter Jennings, Alex Trebeck, William Shatner, Jim Carey, and Dan Akroyd are shining examples of Canadian communicators who have earned celebrity status and millions of dollars.

About 10,000 men and women in Canada hold various kinds of commercial and noncommercial broadcasting jobs. They work at some 750 AM and FM radio stations, which offer a variety of formats (see Table 3.5); nearly 300 television outlets; and numerous cable systems. Additional thousands are employed in such related businesses as computer websites, film and recording studios, syndication services, postproduction facilities, advertising and public relations agencies, public and private video systems, and satellite and wireless networks.

While most electronic media in Canada are financially healthy and offer promising employment opportunities, half the country's radio stations report losing money and want to be deregulated so that owners can have multiple stations and become more efficient, competitive, and profitable.

Table 3.5 Top Radio Formats in Canada

Type of Programming	Number of Stations
1. Adult Contemporary	206
2. Country	158
3. MOR (Middle of the Road)	86
4. Diversified	67
5. Oldies	64
6. Contemporary Hits/Top 40	55
7. News/Talk	40
8. News	26
9. Variety/Diverse	25
10. Classic Rock	25
11. Classical	24
12. Talk	23
13. Public Affairs	17
14. Foreign Language/Ethnic	13
15. Religious	8
TOTAL	837*

*This list represents only stations that participated in the survey and does not include several dozen types of ethnic and musical programming aired part-time in seventeen different foreign languages by various Canadian radio stations.

Source: *Broadcasting and Cable Yearbook*, 1997.

The Canadian Broadcasting Corporation, established by the government and publicly owned, operates nationwide English and French TV and AM-FM stereo networks. The programming is nearly all Canadian and noncommercial. CBC North transmits programs in seven native languages to minority groups in rural areas. Radio Canada International broadcasts shortwave in seven languages around the world. National satellite channels also carry newscasts and programs in multiple languages.

Subscribers to Canadian cable programming services have access to more than thirty networks. They include CBC Newsworld and other networks devoted to home shopping, music, sports, religion, movies, public affairs, homes, gardens, and families.

Canadian commercial radio networks include Radiomutuel Inc. and Telemedia Communications Inc., both headquartered in Montreal. Commercial television networks in Canada are: CTV Television Network Ltd., Global Television Network, TVA, and Television Quatre Saisons.

JOB HUNTING IN CANADA

There are no restrictions on U.S. citizens seeking employment in a Canadian communications facility. Methods of operation, working conditions, equipment, and benefits are similar to those in the United States, but salaries do not average quite as high. Some media jobs in Canada require that you be able to speak both English and French, and it will be helpful to know something about Canadian history, geography, and politics.

Working in Canada can be a satisfying experience, especially if you want to live in a less-crowded environment that offers opportunities for creative expression. Unlike the United States, a number of TV and radio stations in Canada still feature locally produced dramas, comedy, musical concerts, documentaries, discussions, and variety shows.

For more information about jobs, check with employment agencies in principal Canadian cities, surf for Internet job listings, contact individual media employers listed in *Broadcasting & Cable Yearbook,* or ask for help from any of these organizations:

Canadian Association of Broadcasters
Box 627, Station B
306-350 Sparks Street
Ottawa, Ontario K1P 5S2

Canadian Cable Television Association
360 Albert Street, Suite 1010
Ottawa, Ontario K1R 7X7

Canadian Broadcasting Corporation
1500 Bronson Avenue
P. O. Box 8748
Ottawa, Ontario K1G 3J5

Canadian Film and Television Production Association (CFTPA)
N. Tower, 175 Bloor Street E.
Suite 806
Toronto, Ontario M4W 3R8

CHAPTER 4

YOU AND ELECTRONIC MEDIA

The real world of electronic communication is a volatile marketplace, where technology and government deregulation have precipitated many changes recently in ownership and management. It is wise for anyone contemplating a career in radio, television, cable, or any other form of broadcasting or narrowcasting, to be prepared to operate in a highly competitive and somewhat unpredictable environment. If job security is uppermost in your mind, then you should go into another line of work. Most electronic communicators create their own security by being so capable and dependable that their employers consider them indispensable.

Don't consider electronic media as the key to fame and fortune, either. Few jobs in broadcasting and narrowcasting are high-salaried, on-camera positions. Most men and women in the industry are content to work behind the scenes as news, programming, and production professionals; skilled technicians; sales and marketing experts; advertising, promotion, and public relations virtuosos; clerical and craftspeople; supervisors and managers.

As in other professions, the most successful and satisfied employees in electronic media are men and women who are serious about communicating in a clear, correct, and concise fashion. They exhibit creativity and self-reliance, but do so within the boundaries of management's policies and their own sound judgment.

WEIGHING YOUR MEDIA OPTIONS

There are many logical reasons to study and prepare for a career in electronic communication, especially if you are interested in creating and sharing knowledge with other people. This is what communication is all about. The avenues of electronic expression available to you are multiplying rapidly, providing a variety of video and audio channels for interacting with the public in a personal and intimate manner.

A television station can be a stimulating workplace, a vital news-and-information center, and an influential participant in community affairs. As a TV employee, you will get to meet interesting people—newsmakers, celebrities, business executives—and make contacts that might be helpful to your career.

Perhaps you will choose radio as the place to launch your broadcast career. A progressive radio station is in constant contact with listeners throughout its coverage area, and its programming reflects their interests and concerns. Working in this type of operation—reporting hometown happenings; playing local music preferences; sharing the fun of contests, games, and promotions—can make for a job that is richly satisfying.

And there are other options. Job opportunities at websites and cable television are growing along with an expanding list of channels, networks, and cable programming services. Numerous other organizations—TV production studios, educational institutions, advertising and public relations firms, medical facilities, government agencies, public utilities, and private corporations—all employ a sizable number of people in the creation, development, sales, and distribution of video and audio materials.

On the negative side, not all broadcasting stations or video facilities are pleasant places to work. Some are crowded, cluttered, and poorly maintained. Staff members in some instances work long shifts and odd hours for minimal compensation and have little or no job protection.

With deregulation of broadcasting, many owners concentrate on buying and selling stations instead of operating them as a service to the public and a long-term business investment. When a station changes hands, it is not unusual for people to lose their jobs. At some stations, performers get fired if their popularity ratings decline. Discrimination is also a recurring problem in the industry, with women and minorities accusing some employers of inequities in pay and work assignments.

On the other hand, many managers go out of their way to be fair and to retain employees by letting them know they are appreciated. A sizable number of companies pay tuition and expenses for selected personnel to take special courses or attend seminars and conferences. About 40 percent of the nation's broadcast companies have employee pension plans.

When interviewing for a job, it is wise to inquire about employee benefits—particularly medical care, stock options, retirement provisions, and self-improvement classes. Keep in mind, though, it is more important to emphasize the contributions you are prepared to make than to dwell on what an employer has to offer you. Your chances of getting a good job and keeping it will depend primarily on your willingness to give the best that you have to offer, cheerfully and consistently.

ASK THE PROFESSOR

If the prospect of someday being an electronic media professional excites your imagination and curiosity, you should make an effort to find out as much as you can about broadcasting and narrowcasting. Make appointments with communication specialists who have accumulated many years of knowledge and experience. They may be able to help you choose a profession that is suited to your talent and interests by answering questions and concerns that are uppermost on your mind.

Dr. Barry L. Sherman, professor of broadcasting, and director of the Peabody Awards at the University of Georgia, has counseled with hundreds of students about electronic communication careers. Here are his responses to some of the questions he is most often asked:

Q. How can I best prepare for a career in television, cable, radio, or some other form of electronic communication?

A. The best preparation begins with a college degree. Plan to major in mass communication, journalism, speech communication, or broadcasting at a four-year institution whose program ranks high with the Association for Education in Journalism, the Broadcast Education Association, and other academic and professional authorities.

Q. What do colleges offer that's so valuable?

A. In addition to academic instruction, they provide access to a wealth of extracurricular and cocurricular activities. Most modern universities have campus radio and television facilities, campus newspapers and other publications, speech and debate societies, computer labs, free Internet and electronic mail accounts, drama and film groups, and so on. You can learn a lot by taking full advantage of these opportunities.

Q. How important are internships?

A. Most seniors in electronic media complete at least one internship at a broadcast/cable outlet before graduation. These days, simply having a degree isn't enough. Many employers consider an internship a better learning experience than working as a part-time employee.

Q. Are there certain books or courses that you recommend to students of electronic media?

A. Rather than list specific books or courses, let me suggest that to be well prepared you should place equal emphasis on so-called "theory" and "production" courses. Students often spend too much time in classes that focus on entry-level skills, while neglecting study of writing, critical thinking, history, and broad liberal arts subjects. In general, you need course work in media history, technology, law and policy, social impact and effects, production, advertising, and marketing. You also might consider a minor or elective courses in business, political science, speech communication, drama, and international relations.

Q. What technical skills must I develop?

A. All media students should know how to operate basic equipment associated with programming and production at radio and television stations. In addition, it is now necessary to master computer technology, including word processing, digital video and audio editing devices, spreadsheets, graphics, e-mail, website operations, and various other kinds of hardware and software. What's more, you will be expected to keep up with new emerging technology.

Q. Do you advise consulting or networking with media professionals?

A. Yes. Mentoring, networking, and other forms of informal contact are often critical to finding a first job and continuing up the career ladder. As has always been the case, it doesn't hurt to know people in the business who are smart, successful, and willing to share what they know with you.

VALUABLE COMMUNICATION QUALITIES

Emerging technologies continue to change the specifications for various kinds of electronic media jobs. But a basic requirement for all positions is the ability to communicate. Many of the qualities that will enable you to communicate successfully are similar to those that a wise manager should look for when hiring any employee—good work habits, sound judgment, enthusiasm, patience, a sense of humor, empathy, a personal commitment to excellence, and a sincere desire to understand and be understood.

How do you develop these qualities? Some must emanate naturally from your own positive attitude and desire to succeed. Others can be learned through study, observation, and experience. Getting a well-rounded education in both communication courses and the liberal arts will give you knowledge, awareness, and confidence. Working as an intern or trainee will teach you how to use state-of-the-art communication technology and improve your ability to think, speak, and write clearly.

As you prepare for the future, keep an open mind about the direction in which a communication career may lead you. Many students who major in broadcasting don't go to work for a TV or radio station. They find employment in cable operations, production studios, computer systems, nonbroadcast video and audio, satellite delivery, and scores of other businesses.

Colleges of communication are stressing the importance of being versatile and knowing how to do more than one kind of work. As a result, broadcast majors commonly include among their elective courses, classes in computer technology, sales, promotion, advertising, marketing, research, and management.

Knowledge of multiple disciplines will give you an advantage in locating a good job. And continually learning new and better ways to do your job will help you to remain profitably employed. Many employers place more emphasis on how adaptable you are to change than on what you already know.

Accordingly, to enhance your career in communications, you should strive to develop the following sterling characteristics:

1. readiness to accept advice, coaching, feedback, and responsibility
2. willingness to collaborate and cooperate as an interdependent team member
3. ability to analyze and solve problems
4. technical ingenuity and efficiency
5. initiative
6. dependability
7. business acumen and financial management expertise
8. leadership potential

By combining the right qualities with a solid practical education, you can multiply your career opportunities and strengthen your qualifications for moving up to positions of greater responsibility and higher authority.

JOB SATISFACTION

Research findings indicate that most electronic media employees have strong ties of affection for their jobs and dedication to the duties they are hired to perform. They enjoy participating in a high-tech environment, producing and distributing various types of information, entertainment, products, and services to the public.

Interviews conducted with communication professionals indicate a high degree of loyalty to the firms they work for and the industry they represent. This is an impressive endorsement in light of the fact that qualifying for many positions requires considerable talent, education, and experience; yet compensation, benefits, and job security are often less than other businesses offer. Apparently, more important than monetary and material considerations is a strong desire to work with like-minded associates in a dynamic, ever-changing, and vitally important profession.

GIVING THE PUBLIC WHAT IT WANTS

Although electronic media are undergoing profound technical and programming changes, the American people apparently still expect to be provided with certain traditionally basic services.

According to a nationwide study conducted in the fall of 1997 by *Broadcast & Cable* magazine and the International Radio and Television Society, 90 percent of the respondents said that they look to TV primarily for news and information. Next came entertainment, 81 percent; supplying leaders with a way to communicate with the public, 76 percent; educating the public, 68 percent; bringing the nation together, 58 percent; serving as a break from real life, 55 percent; helping shape American culture, 55 percent; and aiding consumers in making purchasing decisions, 48 percent.

Teaching character and values to children and teenagers also was listed as a major media responsibility by 48 percent of the survey participants. Research conducted by the author indicates similar public expectations regarding radio, cable, and Internet websites.

Anyone contemplating a career in broadcasting or narrowcasting should be mindful of these findings. Your success or failure may be determined, to a large extent, by how well you respond to these publicly expressed needs and interests.

ELECTRONIC MEDIA CAREER TEST

Place a check mark under "Yes," "No," or "Not Sure" as you read and consider each statement.

	Yes	No	Not Sure
1. I am keenly interested in TV, radio, cable, and other forms of electronic communication.			
2. I enjoy reading about electronic media.			

	Yes	No	Not Sure
3. I have visited radio, TV, and cable operations.			
4. I know how to operate a camcorder.			
5. I can type and use a word processor.			
6. I know how to use a computer.			
7. I like music and have some musical knowledge.			
8. I listen to radio and watch TV nearly every day.			
9. I like to learn about new technology.			
10. I often check to see what's new on cable channels.			
11. I have sought career advice from one or more communication professionals.			
12. I enjoy meeting and talking with people.			
13. I frequently see and hear things on TV that I would like to change or improve.			
14. Being a TV or radio performer sounds exciting, but I prefer some other kind of electronic media job.			
15. I think I am a creative, "idea" person.			
16. I consider myself to be an attentive listener.			
17. When assigned a task, I make sure to understand how to do it before I start.			
18. I am interested in learning new and better ways of doing things.			
19. I enjoy telling others about things I've learned.			
20. If I have a deadline to meet, I meet it.			

	Yes	No	Not Sure

21. I am striving to become a competent writer.

22. I am trying to learn how to be a good speaker.

23. I do quite well on spelling and geography.

24. When criticized, I listen and try to learn.

25. I enjoy reading both fiction and nonfiction.

26. Listening is as important in communication as talking.

27. I am interested in other people's opinions.

28. I keep up with local, national, and foreign news.

29. I have studied a foreign language.

30. Selling and communicating are related functions.

31. I am inclined to ask a lot of questions.

32. Freedom of press doesn't mean freedom from responsibility for what I say.

33. I have many interests, not just one or two.

34. Excuses are embarrassing, so I try to avoid them.

35. I make written notes of things I have to do.

36. I tend to explain things logically and briefly.

		Yes	No	Not Sure
37.	I usually manage to stay calm under pressure.			
38.	Meeting and chatting with strangers appeals to me.			
39.	Working long hours doesn't bother me.			
40.	I am pretty good at fixing things and making repairs.			
41.	Every employee of a business has a duty to help make it profitable and successful.			
42.	In electronic media—as in any business—the main objective should be to satisfy the customers.			
43.	Making a lot of money is not my greatest ambition.			
44.	All jobs in an organization are related and interdependent.			
45.	I work well without needing close supervision.			
46.	Communication is a sharing and caring process.			
47.	Praise, when I have earned it, is worth more to me than money.			
48.	I am a neat, clean, well-mannered person.			
49.	I can keep a secret.			
50.	As a student, I have received more A's and B's than C's and D's.			
	TOTAL			

(Score 2 points for every "Yes" answer. A score of 75 or more indicates a high degree of aptitude for a career in electronic media.)

CHAPTER 5

PREPARING FOR A CAREER IN ELECTRONIC MEDIA

If you are seriously thinking of pursuing a career in some area of electronic communication, you should waste no time in learning more about all phases of the industry. A number of recently published books listed in Appendix B give detailed information about the ever-expanding world of electronic communication. Reading several of these should be a good starting point in your career preparation. You also should make an effort to observe firsthand the jobs that electronic communicators hold and the work they do. Contact local radio stations, television stations, cable companies, and websites. Request permission to talk with managers and members of their staffs. Ask questions about their operations, and learn how various jobs relate to one another.

Check the telephone book for names of other concerns that are engaged in some form of electronic communication, such as production studios, public and private video systems, and telemarketers. Visit with them, and broaden your knowledge of the interrelated communications facilities in the United States and Canada.

Try to decide what kind of work interests you most and best fits your talents and temperament. Are you inclined toward management, sales, engineering, research, marketing, writing, production, or performance? Once you have made a tentative choice, you can inquire of professionals in that field about how you should go about preparing to do their kind of work.

Regardless of the career choice you make, finding a good job will be easier if you are properly educated and have some on-the-job training or experience. Retaining your position and getting promoted will depend, in large measure, on how well you carry out your daily communication responsibilities.

DEVELOP COMMUNICATION SKILLS

As a professional communicator, you should be capable of exchanging and sharing information and opinions—both written and verbal—in a clear and concise manner. This suggests the wisdom of seriously studying, among other subjects, grammar, composition, and the art of plain talk. Improve your public speaking by joining a debate team or drama club. Experiment with speaking extemporaneously while facing a full-length mirror. Learn how to operate a computer, word processor, tape recorder, and video camera. Get acquainted with other communication technology so that you know what the tools-of-the-trade are and how they are used.

Above all, never stop learning and thinking creatively. All forms of electronic media are looking for persons with bright minds and fresh ideas.

WHAT MANAGEMENT WANTS

Executives in television, cable, radio, and related media look for these qualities in selecting an employee: neat appearance, adequate education and experience, positive attitude, understanding of the industry and "the real world," communication skills, technical knowledge, leadership potential, and an awareness of the importance of sales, marketing, public relations, and financial management.

Radio managers want people who are multitalented. Small staffs and lean budgets favor the job hunter who can not only announce and report news, but also sell advertising, write and produce copy, and operate and maintain electronic equipment.

TV stations, cable, and video systems also are tending to hire persons capable of handling multiple responsibilities. In small operations it is not unusual to work in several different areas such as news, sales, production, computer graphics, traffic, and general maintenance.

Electronic media—like all businesses—would like their employees to know more about economics, money management, research, marketing, sales, computer technology, and the laws of communication.

NEED FOR TECHNICAL TALENT

Although you cannot expect to master every new device that appears on the market, you should try to keep up-to-date on inventions and procedures that could affect your line of work. Computers, for instance, have developed into multimedia machines that incorporate stereo sound, animated graphics, speech, photographs, and text into their programs, along with interactive capabilities. Electronic media use computers to do everything from news preparation, video-audio editing, graphics, automated programming, and bookkeeping to manning a sophisticated telephone switchboard. It will pay you to familiarize yourself with computers and other emerging communication technology.

VERSATILITY IS VALUABLE

Whatever your job interests may be, you should try to develop more than one skill. Broaden your knowledge and become adept at doing a number of different things. This is particularly important in organizations where a few persons take care of all the duties. Tom Ptak is general manager of a small-town radio station in Georgia. He also spends some time each day working as sales manager, program director, announcer, and engineer. When needed, he even helps with bookkeeping, traffic, and "cutting the grass around the tower." It's wise to keep this need for diverse skills in mind as you plan your education.

EDUCATION

High School Preparation

High school is a good place to start preparing for any career. Knowledge and study habits developed in these formative years will prove invaluable as you grow older. Every course that you take will add to your storehouse of usable information, especially courses in English, history, science, mathematics, geography, foreign languages, industrial arts, and social studies.

If you plan to work someday in electronic media, start reading up on the subject. Appropriate books and periodicals can be found in most libraries. Join or organize a communications club. Visit broadcasting stations, cable companies, and related facilities to observe what goes on behind the scenes. Inquire about internships or part-time employment. Nothing beats on-the-job experience.

Trade and Technical Schools

Numerous schools in the United States and Canada offer courses and grant certificates in broadcast engineering; television/radio copywriting, editing, production, sales, announcing, and newscasting; cablecasting; computer science; telecommunications management; video/audio maintenance and repair; communications law; and other related subjects. Courses usually run from six months to a year. An exception, DeVry Institute of Technology has both a four-year program and shorter courses.

Schools of this type vary in the quality of instruction and equipment. Before enrolling in a course, check to see if the institution is accredited by the National Association of Trade and Technical Schools or licensed by a state board of education. Though not as impressive or valuable as a university degree, trade school training has helped many young men and women launch successful careers. Graduates of these schools frequently get jobs with small companies, gain experience, and then move up to better-paying positions.

College and University Training

Although some jobs in electronic media do not require higher education, you will find it much easier to obtain employment and qualify for promotion if you have a degree or at least some college education. Advanced schooling is generally required for supervisory and management positions that carry greater responsibilities and offer bigger salaries.

In today's competitive environment, it also is advisable to take refresher courses periodically. Continuing the educational process will make you more knowledgeable and improve your ability to deal with people and problems. Reading during spare time and attending seminars are other ways to become more proficient.

Some 315 American colleges and universities confer degrees in broadcasting and communication, and at least 1,200 others offer courses in this field of study. Approximately 700 colleges and universities use TV for teaching courses, and 1,100 others rely on television as an instructional supplement.

Students pursuing a degree in communications should balance classes in professional practices with an assortment of liberal arts and technical subjects. It is wise to learn how to operate a computer, word processor, ENG camera, VCR, and fax machine. Some of the subjects that professional broadcasters think students ought to study include: speech, creative writing, current history, psychology, geopolitics, economics, law, marketing, financial management, advertising, public relations, research, sales and sales promotion, and computer graphics.

The Accrediting Council on Education in Journalism and Mass Communications recommends that students obtain a comprehensive background in government and political science, economics, history, geography, sociology, at least one foreign language, and a broad knowledge of English and American literature and composition. The organization also stresses the importance of understanding broadcasting as a social instrument and its relationship to government, industry, and the public.

BROADCASTING FRATERNITIES AND SOCIETIES

Numerous broadcasting and journalistic organizations, dedicated to high standards of education and professionalism, have members or student chapters on college campuses across the country. Among these are the Society of Professional Journalists (Sigma Delta Chi), American Women in Radio and Television (AWRT), Alpha Epsilon Rho (the National Broadcasting Society), Intercollegiate Broadcasting System, Iota Beta Sigma, and National Association of College Broadcasters.

Affiliation with organizations such as these can be an enriching experience, enabling students to meet and make friends with classmates who share common interests and aspirations. After graduating from college, members may elect to affiliate with professional chapters of these organizations.

Selecting a College or University

Schools differ considerably in the type and quality of training they offer. For example, some have modern studios and laboratories with state-of-the-art equipment that allows students to work under actual broadcast conditions. Contrast that with institutions that lack such facilities and must create an imaginary newsroom or studio in an ordinary classroom. Better-endowed schools also are more likely to have faculty members with professional experience. This is preferable to being taught by instructors with only textbook knowledge.

"Look for a university that stresses a real-world environment," advises Terry Likes of Western Kentucky University, "and a program of study that features instructors who have worked in the business."

That real-world environment now means that electronic communications covers a broad spectrum of career options. Acknowledging that many of their students are not destined to work for radio or TV stations, progressive colleges and universities are acquainting students with job opportunities in such areas as cable, production houses, data delivery, computer systems, nonbroadcast video and audio, and satellite communications.

Many colleges have radio stations and television studios. These are excellent places for students to get practical experience by volunteering for work assignments.

Internships, Scholarships, and Fellowships

A sizable number of broadcasters, cable companies, and other electronic media offer students on-the-job training and financial assistance. This aid may be provided as internships, co-op employment, scholarships, fellowships, apprentice positions, or grants for research and study projects related to the industry.

Any student who wants to apply for an internship usually can get details from a school counselor or make direct contact with companies that have such programs. Interns customarily work while on vacation from school. They receive little or no compensation but get valuable experience and a chance to associate with veteran communicators.

Apprentices are usually full-time employees—often disadvantaged youth—who are allowed to earn a salary while learning how to do certain jobs.

Co-op programs at a number of colleges and universities allow students to alternate between attending classes for a semester and doing outside work for a semester. Under this arrangement, participants gain considerable professional experience by the time they receive their diplomas.

Quite a few TV, radio, and cable companies award working scholarships and fellowships. The winners spend a number of weeks working at broadcast stations and cable systems and are paid salaries. Other scholarship awards and financial assistance programs are provided by communication associations, societies, and institutions of higher learning. For details, contact the school that you would like to attend.

HOW TO GET THAT FIRST JOB

"Entry-level positions are not plentiful anywhere in the high-tech communications world, but with proper planning and persistence, jobs can be found," contends James W. Wesley, Jr., former president of Patterson Broadcasting Corp. Here's his advice to young electronic-media job-hunters:

1. *Get a good education and, if possible, professional experience* working part-time or as an intern.
2. *Stay well-informed* by reading books, trade papers, and periodicals about electronic communications. Learn the language of the trade. Keep up with technological progress.
3. *Develop a speciality.* Expertise in computers, consumerism, science, a foreign language, physical fitness, or some other popular subject may give you an advantage in competing for certain jobs where specialized knowledge is needed.

4. *Cultivate industry friends.* Ask for advice from persons experienced in the kind of work you'd like to do. Join a communications club or association. Attend industry meetings, seminars, and conventions. Monitor the media.
5. *Be flexible and adaptable.* Since job responsibilities are not the same in all organizations, keep an open mind about the position you are after. Be willing to meet any reasonable job requirements.
6. *Use a variety of approaches in job hunting.* Consult with school and library career counselors. Check help-wanted ads in industry publications. Contact employment agencies. Rely on networking with people in the business.
7. *Prepare a clean, concise, typed resume,* paying close attention to grammar, spelling, and format. If applicable, put samples of your work on videotape or audiocassette. This can even be material done as classroom assignments. When submitting a resume, attach an appropriate typed letter, which explains briefly why you want the job.
8. *Focus on your objective.* Decide what state or region you prefer to work in and then investigate job opportunities in that area. Don't apply to a large market for a job you're not qualified to handle. Smaller markets are more likely to hire people with limited or no experience, and they provide more diversified training.
9. *Apply with care.* Look for organizations that have a good reputation and are known to be in sound financial condition. Select a few of the most promising, send them letters of application with resumes attached, and ask for an interview. Make sure that the people you are applying to know who you are and what you look like. Face-to-face meetings oftentimes lead to job offers.
10. *Prepare for a job interview* the way the president of the United States gets ready for a news conference. Anticipate what you might be asked and rehearse proper answers. Dress neatly and appropriately. Be prepared to explain how your ability can be of value to the organization you are asking for a job. But don't go overboard and make extravagant claims or promises. Be enthusiastic but modest, confident but respectful.
11. *Employment beats unemployment.* If you can't find a full-time job, look for part-time or temporary employment. Take freelance assignments. This will enable you to earn money and stay active professionally. You're more likely to be offered a job when you are employed than you are if unemployed.
12. *Don't aim too high* or be too demanding. Accept the first reasonable job offer you get. No matter what your ultimate objective is, you must

first get your foot in the door. Be grateful for a modest salary and the chance to gain valuable experience.
13. Finally, *work hard to earn the respect and confidence of your employer,* and be optimistic about the future. If you are determined to be successful, you very likely will be.

RESUMES AND SOFTWARE

A well-crafted resume communicates in a positive and impressive manner an applicant's academic, professional, and personal qualifications for employment. It is one aspect of your job search over which you have complete control, so it behooves you to make your resume neat, easy to read, and logically arranged.

Software is available to simplify resume writing and ensure a letter-perfect manuscript. Using such a program will enable you to create a polished presentation and a good cover letter. It is still advisable, however, to have someone you trust check what you have written for mistakes, omissions, and readability. A poor resume could cost you a job. A well-prepared one may give you the competitive edge you need to be selected for a much-sought-after position.

Software also is available to help you find the kind of work you are best suited for and show you how to prepare for a job interview, including what to wear and what to say and not say. A computer also can give you access to job listings and job-hunting resources.

THE VIDEO RESUME

In applying for an on-air job with a television, cable, or radio station, it is advisable to prepare and submit a video resume. The video resume should be concise but filled with pertinent information about your education, training, and broadcasting experience. Insert clips of your performances on actual programs or newscasts. Don't forget to include your address, phone number, and any other information that might be needed to focus favorably on your qualifications.

Make sure that your resume is accurate and carefully worded, so that it reads well and sounds natural. Rehearse the script until you feel comfortable with its contents and capable of speaking the lines on camera with clarity and authority.

As you prepare to videotape your resume, dress neatly and informally just as you would for an in-person interview. When you go before the camera for the actual production, don't slouch, frown, or try to act funny. Remember to look composed, pleasant, and confident.

While producing the video, stop to redo anything that should be corrected, improved, or deleted. You want the finished product to project your words and your image in the best possible light.

Even if you are looking for an off-camera job, you may want to submit a video resume as an effective method of impressing an employer. This is not advisable, however, if appearing on camera makes you visibly uncomfortable or unable to speak in a clear, calm, and convincing manner.

Applicants for Internet employment may find it helpful to prepare and submit a multimedia resume that demonstrates a combination of journalistic, artistic, video, and audio capabilities. But before sending any kind of video resume, find out if the employer has the technology to view and consider this type of presentation.

LICENSING

The FCC has liberalized or eliminated licensing requirements for many jobs in radio, television, and other electronic media. A professional technician still must qualify for a general operator's license by passing an FCC test, but on-air personnel no longer need a restricted operator's permit. Such permits, however, are still available and can be obtained from any FCC field office. No test is required. For more information about FCC rules, regulations, and license requirements, contact the FCC Call Center, Gettysburg, Pennsylvania, (888) 225-5322.

JOB-HUNTING TIPS

One of the best ways to find a good broadcasting job is through personal contact with people in the business. Cultivate friendships with successful professionals. Seek their advice. If there's a particular organization you want to work for, arrange to visit its headquarters. Spend time learning about its operations and meeting some of its employees.

Commercial firms, government agencies, educational institutions, and professional associations use a variety of media to recruit personnel, including printed ads, website messages, and recorded job hot lines. Classified ads in newspapers and communication periodicals list numerous attractive broadcasting and narrowcasting jobs. It is advisable to check these sources regularly.

More than a million job openings are listed daily on some 5,000 Internet sites. A typical help-wanted ad gives a brief description of the position to be filled, the salary range and benefits, along with required education, skills, and experience. For more information about how to utilize Internet employment sites, consult *The National Job Hotline Directory,* edited by Marcia P. Williams and Sue A. Cubbage, McGraw-Hill, 1996, and the *Electronic Job Search Almanac–1997,* published by Adams Media Corp.

The Georgia Association of Broadcasters and similar groups in other states maintain free employment services. The Society of Professional Journalists and a number of other broadcasting and news associations publish job listings in their journals and on the Internet.

Colleges and universities customarily provide graduates with useful employment and career-advancement guidance. Web surfing is a convenient way to link up with colleagues and find out about employment opportunities. Another way to learn about job openings is to attend meetings of media professionals. Make networking a part of your daily job-hunting routine.

Many communities operate employment offices, hold job fairs, and provide job-counseling services. Help also is available from state and federal employment agencies. Strategic use of these job-locating resources may lead you to a satisfying job and a successful broadcasting career.

PATHWAY TO PROMOTION

Starting pay for most electronic media jobs is modest. But the amount you earn initially is not as important as getting an opportunity to launch your career. Promotions and pay raises will come in time as you earn them. To qualify for recognition and rewards, follow this daily routine:

1. Wake up each morning with a positive attitude.
2. Don't think about working but about being useful, constructive, and helpful to others.
3. Ask questions and listen carefully to the answers.
4. Seek feedback from your bosses, co-workers, and respected professionals.
5. Take care of your health, hair, teeth, nails, and character.
6. Be friendly, cooperative, and trustworthy.
7. Do all that you're supposed to, and more.
8. Profit from your mistakes by not repeating them.

9. Build and safeguard a reputation for dependability.
10. Respect those you work with and those you compete against.
11. Make every day a learning and growing experience.
12. Refrain from volunteering unrequested criticism.
13. Master the machines of your profession.
14. Set short-term and long-term goals, and meet your deadlines for reaching them.
15. Be patient, cheerful, confident, and persistent.
16. Earn the confidence of your superiors.
17. Demonstrate leadership by being a problem solver.
18. Expect good things to happen, and eventually they will.

CHAPTER 6

ELECTRONIC MEDIA—REWARDS AND BENEFITS

As you ponder the possibility of becoming a broadcaster or narrowcaster, it is logical to ask some basic questions: What jobs are available? How do you qualify for them? How much money can you make? Will you be eligible for any special rewards or benefits? Are you likely to be proud and satisfied working as an electronic communicator? Answers to these concerns are generally positive and encouraging.

Employers are looking for qualified applicants to fill job openings at all levels in radio, television, cable, and computer systems. There is demand for specialists in sales, marketing, advertising, news reporting and editing, production, promotion, engineering, digital services, research, accounting, videography, public relations, computer graphics, human resources, and general management.*

A career in electronic media holds promise of both tangible and intangible rewards. Some communication moguls like Ted Turner, Rupert Murdoch, and Bill Gates have amassed enormous fortunes. But they are the exception. Most media professionals are content just to make a comfortable living. More important than money is the knowledge that they are engaged in an interesting and vitally important profession.

Humans are the dominant species on this planet because we communicate, we share and accumulate information and knowledge that makes possible all scientific and social progress. Keep this in mind as you weigh your career options.

---

*Source: *Broadcasting & Cable,* Jan. 12, 1998.

THE EMPLOYMENT OUTLOOK

Jobs in the nation's radio and television stations have always been limited in number because most facilities operate with relatively few people. Automation may further reduce the total of such jobs in coming years. But employment prospects in other forms of electronic media look promising.

As cable channels continue to multiply and offer viewers more choices, there should be a need for additional people to write, produce, market, and promote programs and features. With millions of PC owners surfing the web night and day, the Internet continues to grow and need more communication specialists. Organizations of every kind are establishing websites and using them to advertise and sell ideas, products, and services. This vigorous activity is expected to escalate during the twenty-first century, intensifying demand for multimedia professionals. Similar expansion appears likely in other kinds of wired, wireless, and satellite systems.

Jobs are plentiful for electronic media professionals in advertising, public relations, video production, sales, marketing, promotion, and businesses that operate in-house or network communication systems. Schools and colleges are seeking qualified educators to teach communication courses and manage broadcasting facilities.

Perhaps the most exciting prospects are for job growth in communication technology that combines the capabilities of radio, TV, telephone, videodisks, and other traditional consumer electronics. In development now are voice-activated digital devices that will be able to duplicate the functions of virtually every common communication medium currently used in homes and offices. It is tempting to believe that such scientific marvels will create a huge new job market.

WORKING CONDITIONS*

Electronic media in the United States generally maintain well-equipped, attractive workplaces. Offices and studios are usually neat, modern, and air-conditioned. Most operations have lounges and dining areas where food and refreshments are available. Some even maintain physical-fitness rooms and libraries. Free parking is another common perquisite.

A number of companies sponsor and support employee clubs, softball and bowling teams, and other activities designed to boost morale and promote a

---

*Sources: NAB-BCFM Employee Compensation and Fringe Benefits Report, 1997, plus personal surveys by author.

cooperative family spirit. Staff members are often encouraged to participate in community affairs and contribute leadership to civic, cultural, and charity projects.

The forty-hour week—standard in the electronic communication industry—is normally divided into five eight-hour days. Broadcast performers, however, sometimes work six days a week. Split shifts have decreased, but overtime assignments are common.

Most companies grant one week of vacation after six months of employment. This increases to two weeks after a full year, three weeks after five years, and four weeks after fifteen years. There is no standard or universal plan regarding incentives and fringe benefits. Nearly all broadcasting companies allow eight days of paid sick leave annually. A sizable number provide full or partial payment for life insurance, accidental death, dental care, and short- and long-term disability.

Some employers underwrite the cost of awarding a limited number of civic club and professional-association memberships. Many stations also pay tuition for key employees to attend seminars, workshops, and conventions.

MONEY MATTERS

Those who go job-hunting in the competitive world of electronic media should do so for reasons other than getting rich. You can make money easier and quicker in other professions. Even starting salaries for schoolteachers, generally considered to be low, average well above what a typical beginner in broadcasting and narrowcasting receives. However, capable communicators can make a comfortable living, and quite a few become wealthy.

Something other than money, however, motivates most of the men and women who work as electronic media professionals. Although aware that they could earn more in other fields, many newcomers elect to become communicators because it's what they've had a lifelong desire to do. That should be a primary consideration for anyone when deciding on a career.

Nevertheless, since salaries are a life-sustaining necessity, the tables that follow provide specific information about compensation levels for various electronic media jobs.

Table 6.1 Television Compensation Department Heads

Position	National Average Pay (Salary + Bonus)	Median (Base)	Small Station*	Medium Size Station**	Large Station***
General Manager	$190,000	$151,000	$84,000	$200,000	$290,000
Station Manager	105,000	79,000	59,000	120,000	167,000
Operations Manager	60,000	48,000	39,000	65,000	79,000
Program Director	54,000	40,000	27,000	53,500	75,000
Chief Engineer	65,000	55,000	30,500	68,000	85,000
News Director	83,000	66,000	34,500	80,000	127,000
Marketing Director	70,000	53,000	37,000	61,000	80,000
Promotion/Publicity Director	50,000	39,000	27,000	47,000	71,500
Production Manager	45,000	38,000	30,000	48,000	58,000
Controller	65,000	32,000	34,000	65,000	90,000
Traffic Manager	37,000	31,000	23,500	36,000	46,000
Community Affairs Director	45,000	36,000	21,500	35,000	51,500
Art Director	43,000	37,000	25,000	34,000	49,000
Research Director	45,000	40,000	24,000	38,000	47,000
Human Resources Director	49,000	37,000	35,000	39,000	49,500

*Small market stations—net revenue under $2 million
**Medium-size market stations—net revenue $10–20 million
***Large market stations—net revenue $20–50 million

Sources: 1997–98 salary estimates are composite figures based on research conducted by the Radio/Television News Directors Association, the National Association of Broadcasters/Broadcast Financial Management Association, the Georgia Association of Broadcasters, and the author.

Table 6.2 TV Sales Management

Position	Average Salary (All Markets)	Average Other Compensation (All Markets)	Small Market* Average Salary + Other Compensation	Large Market*** Average Salary + Other Compensation
General Sales Manager	$90,000	$40,000	$49,000 + 21,000	$127,000 + 54,000
Local Sales Manager	70,000	30,000	43,000 + 8,000	95,000 + 36,000
National Sales Manager	70,000	30,000	50,500 + 15,500	91,000 + 33,000
Sales Service/Coop Coordinator	45,000	10,000	18,000 + 1,000	72,000 + 19,000
Account Executive	60,000	§	31,000 §	80,000 §

*Small market station—net revenue under $2 million
***Large market station—net revenue $20–50 million
§No extra compensation reported for account executives

Sources: 1997–98 estimates based on the National Association of Broadcasters/Broadcast Financial Management Association nationwide station surveys and personal research by the author.

Table 6.3 TV Support Staff

Position	Average No. Full-Time Employees	Average Starting Salary	Average Salary (All Markets)	Average Salary (Small Markets)*	Average Salary (Large Markets)***
Operator/Technician	9	$20,000	$27,000	$17,000	$ 37,500
Maintenance Technician	4	27,000	36,000	25,000	45,000
Technical Director	3	24,000	29,000	21,000	37,000
Floor Director	2	21,000	27,000	21,000	33,000
Film/Tape Editor	3	22,000	28,000	20,000	33,000
Film Director	1	24,000	30,000	26,500	41,000
News Anchor	5	38,000	73,000	21,000	121,000
News Reporter	7	25,000	35,000	18,000	53,000
News Photographer	8	22,500	28,000	19,500	39,000
Sportscaster	2	30,000	54,000	21,000	86,000
Weathercaster	2	32,000	55,000	29,000	42,000
Assignment Editor	2	26,000	34,000	25,000	38,000
Production Assistant	3	17,000	20,000	16,500	24,000
Staff Artist	2	23,500	30,000	24,500	34,000
Traffic/Computer Operator	3	17,000	23,000	17,000	25,000
Producer/Director	4	24,000	33,000	26,500	41,000

*Small market stations—net revenue under $2 million
***Large market stations—net revenue $20–50 million

Sources: 1997–98 salaries are composite figures based on surveys of U.S. commercial TV stations conducted by the National Association of Broadcasters/Broadcast Financial Management Association and personal research by the author.

Table 6.4 Radio Salaries

Position	National Average (Salary + Other Compensation)	Median (Base Salary)	Small Station*	Medium Station*	Large Station***
General Manager	$180,000	$124,000	$108,000	$127,500	$239,000
General Sales Manager	116,000	78,000	67,000	86,000	152,000
Local Sales Manager	95,000	69,000	65,000	69,000	108,000
National Sales Manager	98,000	66,000	60,000	90,000	104,000
New Business Development/Coop Vendor	68,000	61,000	45,000	48,000	75,000
Account Executive (highest)	99,000	94,000	52,000	74,000	130,000
Account Executive (2nd highest)	79,000	76,000	40,000	57,000	105,000
Account Executive (average of others)	50,000	47,000	27,000	37,000	60,000
Program Director	70,000	68,000	46,000	53,000	120,000
Programming Assistant	30,000	27,500	22,500	28,000	30,000
Morning Drive Talent	100,000	66,000	49,000	54,000	145,000
Morning Drive Producer	29,000	25,000	26,000	22,500	35,000
Midday Talent	43,000	35,000	29,000	35,000	62,000
Afternoon Drive Talent	55,000	39,000	34,000	35,000	85,000
Evening Talent	35,000	27,000	22,000	23,000	45,000
Late Night Talent	25,000	20,000	17,000	19,000	35,000
Production Director	40,000	38,000	27,500	30,000	46,000
Music Director/Assistant Production Director	40,000	36,500	22,000	25,000	48,000

Research Director	42,000	31,000	21,500	22,500	48,000
News Director	44,000	38,500	23,500	29,500	56,000
News Reporter	35,000	27,500	15,000	21,500	38,000
News Announcer	34,000	27,000	22,500	22,000	51,000
Sports Director	46,000	37,500	16,000	30,000	45,000
Auto Traffic Reporter	38,000	30,000	15,000	23,000	31,000
Promotion Director	38,000	34,000	23,000	27,000	48,000
Promotion Assistant	24,000	22,000	17,000	22,000	26,000
Director Traffic Department	30,000	28,500	20,000	23,500	35,000
Continuity Director	27,000	26,000	15,000	18,000	28,000
Chief Engineer	50,000	48,000	35,000	36,000	60,000
Business Manager/Controller	47,000	44,000	36,500	38,000	65,000
Assistant Business Manager	31,000	30,500	20,000	25,000	33,000
Sales Assistant	24,000	23,500	18,000	21,000	25,000
Receptionist	19,000	18,500	15,000	16,000	20,000

*Small market stations—net revenue under $2 million
**Medium-size market stations—net revenue $10–20 million
***Large market stations—net revenue $20–50 million

Sources: 1997–98 radio salaries are composite figures based on surveys conducted by the National Association of Broadcasters/Broadcast Financial Management Association, Radio/Television News Directors Association, *Broadcast Engineering* magazine, and the author.

Table 6.5 Cable System Salaries
Salaries vary depending on system size
and number of subscribers

Position	Salary Range
Cable System General Manager	$ 60,000 to 275,000
Regional General Manager	100,000 to 175,000
Regional Controller	80,000 to 120,000
Regional Advertising/Sales Manager	65,000 to 90,000
System Advertising/Sales Manager	35,000 to 50,000
Advertising/Sales Representative	13,000 to 25,000
Regional Marketing Manager	60,000 to 95,000
System Marketing Manager	35,000 to 60,000
Local Marketing Specialist	25,000 to 50,000
Systems Chief Engineer	45,000 to 75,000
Technical Operations Manager	40,000 to 80,000
Installation Manager/Supervisor	30,000 to 60,000
Head End Microwave Technician	30,000 to 40,000
Senior Installer	20,000 to 30,000
Installer	16,300 to 22,000
Customer Service Trainer	30,000 to 50,000
Office/Business Manager	30,000 to 50,000
Customer Service Manager/Trainer	30,000 to 40,000
Customer Service Representative	18,000 to 25,000
Traffic Coordinator	20,000 to 30,000
Programming Manager	30,000 to 60,000
Producer/Director	20,000 to 40,000
Production Assistant	18,000 to 20,000
Camera Operator	15,000 to 25,000
Announcer/Performer	15,000 to 50,000
News/Weather Reporter	15,000 to 50,000

Source: Salary ranges are 1998 estimates based on pay scales at small, medium, and large cable systems throughout the United States.

CHAPTER 7

RADIO JOBS

Radio is so universally popular and necessary that nearly everyone in the United States does some listening each day. The personal nature of radio broadcasting makes any job in this field a challenging one. People who work in radio are not isolated observers or detached reporters of the current scene; they are participants with a large following of listeners in a unique kind of communication process. This develops out of the way that radio works—reaching the mind and stirring the imagination through the sense of sound—making for an intimate, one-to-one relationship.

It may well be that the greatest service provided by radio is the companionship that this localized, mobile, around-the-clock community service provides in the form of news, music, conversation, commentary, humor, and a host of other types of information and inspiration. It is well documented that radio stations take on a personality of their own and frequently enjoy the friendship and loyalty of a vast audience. The most respected station is one at which staff members are deeply involved in the life of the community and reflect this involvement in a variety of attractive and reliable broadcast services.

Many progressive minds in radio have worked to create a dynamic industry that changes constantly to match the needs and desires of the public. There is a profound difference between the sound of today's radio commercials and those that were heard twenty-five years ago. The same is true of radio music, news, and talk—programs are much more frank, explicit, and informal than they were a generation ago. Understandably, jobs in radio also have changed. Gone are the days of the stuffy announcer, the likeable but ignorant salesperson, or the engineer who thought only technically and not in human terms.

Radio is, in many ways, the most versatile, adaptable, and efficient of all the media. In its ability to reach and cater to a multitude of people with instantaneous and ever-changing local service, it is unique. Anyone who makes radio broadcasting a career choice should understand these characteristics of the medium and be prepared to work comfortably and energetically in a profession that emphasizes speed, flexibility, spontaneity, and close contact with the audience.

There always has been a need in radio for people who are talented, sensitive, dependable, and of good character. But the progress of broadcasting calls for more than this. Radio needs imaginative and competitive communicators who believe in the medium and its mission. Radio needs young men and women who want to stay and build a career, rather than use radio as a stepping-stone to an eventual spot in television or another field.

Although job titles and duties may vary somewhat, the basic functions of radio operations are quite similar, regardless of the size of the station or its staff. This makes it possible for a beginner to learn broadcasting fundamentals at a small station and later transfer these skills to a bigger station in a larger market, where compensation and working conditions may be more attractive. Such a move upward is most likely to succeed if the employee has concentrated on gaining valuable experience and has absorbed a great deal of practical, on-the-job know-how about the many facets of broadcasting.

GROUP AND NICHE PROGRAMMING

Specialized formats predominate in the programming of commercial radio stations in the United States. Most stations transmit and promote a single type of music, designed to appeal to a certain demographic or psychographic segment of the local population. A sizable number of facilities play no music at all, offering instead all talk, news and talk, or sports.

Microformatting, especially of music, also is common in Canada and other countries. This simple, tightly controlled, niche programming is favored by owners and managers for four reasons: it sells, it can be automated, it requires fewer people, and it can be adapted for use by a group of stations. Multiple station ownership is increasing and has resulted in the elimination of jobs and even departments, such as news and weather.

Consolidation of ownership isn't all bad though. More high-salaried positions have opened up for specialists in intermarket programming, syndication, mini-networks, group sales, and promotion.

Despite rapid growth of other electronic media, radio remains strong and popular. Studies indicate that Americans still depend heavily on radio at home, at work, and in their automobiles. One outlet is often preferred over others because it has "the best music," "the funniest disk jockeys," or "the most reliable news, weather, and traffic."

Relatively few stations continue to provide diversified entertainment, advice, and information. The vast majority now try to fill a specific programming niche so expertly that they are able to outperform all competitors in this one narrowly focused area. Revenues nationwide indicate positive results from their efforts. The industry is healthy and new stations are steadily being licensed to go on the air.

But radio is a medium that has always attracted restless and innovative communicators. In the next century we will very likely listen to many new kinds of niche programming. Maybe you will be one of those who helps to create an era of fresh audio sounds and services.

AUTOMATION AND SYNDICATION

Thousands of radio stations are now semi-automated or completely automated. Computerized systems regulate the flow of program elements. Networks, program producers, and format providers supply music, talk, news, and features for these mechanized operations. According to the owner of two stations that are programmed entirely by satellite: "With our computers, and voice tracks, we are using minimum-wage employees to sit and push the appropriate buttons. But we sound live and local!" This trend toward automation is reducing the demand for announcers, newspeople, and other staff talent. Most such opportunities are now to be found only in FM and AM stations that continue to originate their own programming.

Syndicated program distribution by satellite, wireless, or other means is a thriving business. Scores of firms are engaged in program production, marketing, merchandising, and bartering. Barter inventory consists of programming or services that syndicators trade to broadcasters in exchange for commercial airtime. The syndicator then sells the bartered airtime to advertisers.

Numerous jobs are available in the syndication industry, especially for persons experienced in sales and marketing. There are opportunities as well in developing programs for syndication.

DOLLARS AND SENSE

If the prospect of building a career in radio sounds intriguing and you would like to know more about this form of broadcasting, you should talk with successful leaders in the profession such as Michael McDougald. Five years after graduating from Emory University, he bought the first of many radio stations. Now, more than a half century later, the award-winning president of McDougald Broadcasting Co., answers some questions that students often ask.

Q. Are broadcasting jobs scarce or plentiful?

A. Although a lot of properties are changing hands and downsizing, job prospects are generally pretty good for positions in management, sales, programming, news, and engineering. Many of the unfilled spots exist at small-market stations, where working conditions are usually pleasant but salary levels do not match those paid by large-market operations.

Q. Can I be a successful broadcaster without a college education?

A. Yes, but it does help to have a degree in communication and to take courses in broadcasting, journalism, sales, marketing, and computer technology. However, there's much you can and should learn on your own about the broadcasting industry's history, present status, and probable future.

Q. Is it wise to start in a small market?

A. There's no better place to get all-around experience. Big stations in large markets are reluctant to hire and train novices, but a small-market operation will welcome you if you are willing to work long hours for a small salary, and they'll give you plenty of opportunities to learn and grow.

Q. What jobs are most plentiful?

A. All electronic media are looking for salespeople. Many small radio operations are seeking personalities to preside over morning and afternoon drive shows. TV news departments have a continuing need for reporters, photographers, and engineers. Radio and TV announcers are less in demand because so many stations now rely on automation and satellite feeds for much of their programming. Office jobs such as traffic, bookkeeping, and receptionist, are usually easy to find if you know how to use computers and other timesaving technology.

Q. Why so much emphasis on technology?

A. Because technology is the driving force that will lead the communication industry into the next millennium. Broadcasters must understand this in order to survive and prosper. To qualify for most electronic media jobs you should have some degree of technical know-how. It's virtually standard procedure in program, sales, and news departments to "do things" with computers, faxes, satellites, scanners, e-mail, modems, and other kinds of digital machines.

Q. What broadcasting jobs pay the best?

A. Sales is where the money is. A person who likes to sell and knows how to do it well can always find employment, and be well compensated. Regrettably, a lot of intelligent and capable men and women are reluctant or afraid to try selling anything. I have attempted many times to make account executives out of announcers, engineers, programmers, and office personnel, only to find that most of them aren't really interested in mastering the art of selling and serving the needs of advertisers. They lack the stamina, patience, and willingness to accept rejection without admitting defeat. Good salespeople are valuable, and they often make more money than anyone else in the company, including the manager.

Q. Are salaries about the same for comparable jobs in radio, television, cable, and the Internet?

A. Pay scales vary with the size of the operations. The bigger the organization and the larger the market, the higher your paycheck is likely to be. But the cost of living in a larger market also will be higher.

Q. What other good advice can you give me?

A. Don't expect too much too soon. I frequently interview vain, lackadaisical clock-watchers, who have grown up feeling that somebody owes them a fine job with virtually no responsibilities. Even college graduates, with little or no experience, often assume that a diploma entitles them to start making a whopping salary on the day they are hired. Broadcasting offers many benefits and rewards, but they must be earned.

PROGRAMMING AND PRODUCTION

Positions available in radio programming and production include the following:

Program Director. Wherever a radio station originates its own programming, the person responsible for giving the station a popular and distinctive sound is the program director. Working with announcers and other staff members, the PD develops programming targeted toward a particular demographic audience that both the station and its advertisers want to reach.

In many stations the program director also serves as an announcer, salesperson, satellite-and-computer coordinator, or assistant station manager. At some locations the job entails handling community affairs, automated operations, and personnel matters. The program director of a large station is usually expected to have knowledge of sales, marketing, research, strategic planning, promotion, and budgeting.

Prerequisites include a college degree, preferably in communications; several years of broadcast experience; technical, creative, and leadership skills; and management potential. Salaries range from $40,000 to $300,000, depending on market size. The national average is about $70,000.

Assistant Program Director. This position is often held by a senior staff member who assists the program director in discharging the duties of the program department. To qualify, you should have college training and professional experience in programming, sales, and marketing. Salaries range from $25,000 to $35,000.

Music Director. This is an important position in stations that select the songs and artists that are played. Instead of making arbitrary choices, however, the MD is likely to rely heavily on demographic research, record sales figures, and music popularity charts in deciding what numbers to pick. Many stations no longer have a music director. They contract with companies that supply around-the-clock musical programming on tape or by satellite delivery. To qualify as a music director, you need to know how to select songs that fit a station's format and how to play them by computerized sequencing. Broadcast experience is helpful. The national average salary for a music director is $30,000, but some make $50,000 to $100,000.

Radio Operations Director/Production Manager. The job title may vary, but the position entails coordinating the creative output of the program, sales, news, and technical departments to make sure that all the station's programs and commercials are properly produced. Duties may include assigning announcers and producers; troubleshooting production problems; supervising the operation and maintenance of studios, production equipment, and vehicles; and endeavoring to make the station's overall programming sound as good as possible.

A liberal arts education, broadcast production experience, and demonstrated management potential are prerequisites for this job.

Salaries range from $15,000 to $20,000 in small markets to $50,000 to $75,000 in major ones. The national average salary is about $40,000.

Radio Producer/Director. This job is found most often in radio stations that require a coordination director for morning and afternoon drive-time programs, two-way talk shows, or other programs that require a producer to book guests, screen phone calls, and integrate news, traffic reports, and features into a fast-moving format. Off-air, producers write and produce commercials and promotional announcements. On shows that use such material, they also often write skits, scan publications for program ideas, suggest publicity stunts and contests, and localize news stories—adapting ideas used in other areas to their own market. At small stations with simple formats, announcers and disc jockeys serve as their own producers.

The job of producer-director at larger stations usually is held by a senior staff member with considerable experience in announcing, writing, news, and commercial production.

Salaries run from $25,000 to $110,000. The national average is $29,000.

Programming/Production Assistant. The holder of this position assists the program and production departments. Duties may include serving as director of community affairs and responding to inquiries, requests for assistance, and cooperation on community events and projects. This job also may entail scheduling public service programs and announcements and maintaining records of services rendered to civic groups, schools, religious organizations, charities, and minorities.

To best fill this position you should have a communication degree and be interested in public affairs and community service. A salary of $20,000 to $35,000 is common. The national average is about $30,000.

DISK JOCKEYS AND DRIVE-TIME TALENT

Millions of listeners dial to specific radio stations every day because they prefer to hear certain personalities. Some are hosts of music shows. Others preside over news and talk programs, interviewing guests and chatting about topical subjects, both light and serious. Morning drive-time is the most valuable period of the broadcast day. Announcers who work these hours normally make the most money. Afternoon drive is the next most important time, followed by nighttime and late night segments.

Disk jockeys who feature primarily a specific type of music should be friendly and possess a keen sense of humor, a pleasant voice, a good education, and a warm, engaging manner. Talk-show talent needs to be keenly aware of current affairs and adept at discussing any issues or hot topics that the audience wants to sound off about.

Salaries for air-talent range from a small-town low of $17,000 to $750,000 or more in major markets.

GENERAL ANNOUNCERS

Relatively few persons are now employed exclusively as radio announcers. Instead, an employee who can read intelligently and speak clearly may be assigned multiple duties that include announcing, writing and producing commercials, reporting, interviewing, newscasting, and sales. Salaries range from $15,000 to $50,000.

MORNING-DRIVE RADIO SALARIES

Pay for announcers on morning-drive radio programs varies considerably, depending upon the size of the market, how the stations are formatted, and the popularity of the talent. The following salary averages range from very low in small communities to exceedingly high in large cities.

Morning-Drive Radio Format	Average Pay for Talent	Median	Low	High
AOR	$150,000	$105,000	$16,000	$775,000
Adult Contemporary	95,000	60,000	13,000	600,000
Sports Talk	35,000	33,000	27,000	45,000
Nostalgia/Big Band	56,000	51,000	22,000	150,000
Soft "Lite" AC	80,000	55,000	16,000	325,000
Urban Contemporary	97,000	46,000	16,000	450,000
Contemporary Hit (CHR)	105,000	72,000	22,000	650,000
Country	95,000	67,000	23,000	620,000
News/Talk	120,000	75,000	25,000	800,000
Spanish	62,000	50,000	16,000	250,000
Classical	60,000	35,000	25,000	110,000
New Rock	50,000	37,000	22,000	150,000
Full Service AM	120,000	100,000	40,000	325,000
Easy Listening	65,000	50,000	15,000	215,000
Classic Rock	110,000	65,000	19,000	475,000

Source: Research findings of the National Association of Broadcasters, various broadcasting publications, and the author, 1997.

SUPERSTARS

Sometimes a disk jockey, talk-show host, or commentator becomes popular enough to be recognized as a celebrity. Performers of this caliber frequently generate a high percentage of a station's revenue. Paul Harvey and Rush Limbaugh generate millions in sales for their networks. Early in their careers, Larry King, Dick Clark, and Sally Jesse Raphael worked as radio station announcers and learned showmanship fundamentals that helped them to become famous and successful. Few radio performers ever qualify as superstars, but many local personalities are highly popular and well paid. They excel at what they do by working hard and being consistently well informed and more interesting than their competitors. If you are uniquely talented and know how to entertain in a superior manner, you still can strike it rich in radio.

SALES

The American system of commercial radio broadcasting is based on a simple premise: attracting listeners with entertainment and information: then "selling" that audience of listeners to advertisers. This sales effort has become a sophisticated process involving the unified efforts of management, air personalities, producers, promotional experts, and salespeople. Together they market the station's tightly formatted sound and service by utilizing demographic data and consumer research, innovative marketing concepts, sales and audience promotion, strong merchandising, and extensive use of other media for advertising and publicity.

Radio revenues comes from five principal advertising sources: local, regional, national, co-op, and network. The first four are sold by the station's sales staff or its sales representatives. Network compensation comes from broadcasting commercials or programs sold by a network.

Positions available in radio sales include the following:

General Sales Manager. This person is the leader of the radio station's sales and marketing team. He or she must be able to recruit, train, and motivate a capable and competitive sales force; identify revenue opportunities; and maximize income. Prerequisites: a business or communication degree and a record of success in sales and management.

Compensation may be by salary, commission, bonus, or any combination of these. Radio sales managers earn anywhere from $60,000 to $250,000 a year. The national average is $116,000.

Local Sales Manager. The local sales manager is responsible for local advertising revenue. He or she supervises concept-marketing efforts of the local sales staff and may handle some accounts personally. This job is usually filled by someone who was promoted from the sales staff. Average earnings nationwide are $95,000. The best ones make more than $125,000.

National Sales Manager. The national sales manager is responsible for national advertising revenue. He or she works with the station's national sales representatives to solicit and obtain orders from major multicity advertisers. Average compensation for this job is $98,000.

Account Executive/Salesperson. The account executive/salesperson makes sales-and-marketing presentations to businesses and advertising agencies. Duties in small stations may include writing, announcing, and producing commercials after selling them. A college education is desirable, especially courses in advertising, marketing, research, and psychology.

Earnings may come from commissions only or a combination of salary and commission. Account execs average $50,000 a year, but incomes of $100,000 or more are not uncommon for smart, hard workers.

Sales-Support Person. This person provides assistance to the sales managers and account executives—secretarial duties, word processing, record keeping. Average salary for this job is $24,000.

Sales Specialists. These are persons who specialize in generating one particular type of radio revenue. Examples include:

Co-op Coordinator. This job requires finding out where co-op advertising funds, allocated by major suppliers, are available. Then the coordinator persuades eligible local firms to spend the money on radio. National average compensation for this job is $68,000.

Sports Sales Specialist. This specialist sells sports sponsorships and commercials for sports events and programs. One big radio station in Atlanta pays its sports marketer more than $100,000 a year in commissions.

Radio Continuity Director/Copywriter. This person conceives and writes commercial announcements and other copy, often rapidly and under pressure. Ability to direct and record commercials is another requirement in many stations. Prerequisites are a college degree with emphasis on English, advertising, and broadcasting courses. Average salary is less than $20,000, but experienced professionals usually make $35,000 to $45,000.

Radio Merchandising Manager. The merchandising manager helps advertisers sell their products and services with point-of-purchase displays, sales incentives, on-air contests, sales promotional mailings, and other forms of support and encouragement. Prerequisites for the job are a degree in business or communication, plus training or experience in sales, advertising, and promotion. Salary range is $25,000 to $50,000.

MARKETING, PROMOTION, AND PUBLICITY

Radio stations use a variety of marketing and promotional techniques to project a distinctive personality and sound-image, and to attract listeners and advertisers with their programming, performers, popularity, and sales power. These efforts involve the use of multimedia and fall into a number of categories—audience promotion, sales promotion, merchandising, publicity, and public relations.

Marketing Director/Promotion Director. He or she supervises the station's marketing efforts, working closely with sales, programming, research, promotion, and publicity departments. The director also creates comprehensive sales and audience-building campaigns. Minimum job requirements are a bachelor's degree with courses in broadcasting, advertising, and promotion; strong creative, strategic, and competitive talents; and experience in broadcast promotion. National average salary is $38,000. The salary range is $25,000 to $80,000.

Marketing/Promotion Assistant. Duties may include working on publicity releases, radio-TV promotional announcements, advertising campaigns, contests, stunts, special events, merchandising tie-ins, and research projects. A degree in communication with courses in advertising and public relations is advisable; word-processing skills are also a plus. Starting salary for marketing/promotion assistants is about $17,000. National average salary is $24,000.

RESEARCH

Research has become increasingly important to broadcasters who want to be continually updated on the popularity of music, air personalities, programs, and the relative strength of their competition. Some stations have research directors on their staffs and use research findings for sales and marketing campaigns, but most stations contract with research firms to obtain needed information. Thousands of stations subscribe to Arbitron, Birch, and other research companies for periodic audience-measurement reports.

Research Director. He or she obtains and analyzes information needed by broadcasters in making programming, sales, and advertising decisions. Needed to qualify: an undergraduate degree in business administration with emphasis on computerized demographic, psychographic, and marketing research. Experience in radio sales or programming is helpful. Nationwide salary average is $42,000. Large operations pay up to $85,000.

MANAGEMENT AND ADMINISTRATION

In every radio station a staff of administrators and their assistants provides leadership, guidance, and support to all employees and every department. At the top are the owners and managers. Backing them up are specialists in finance, human resources, office services, maintenance, and security. Included in the general administrative family are secretaries, switchboard operators, clerks, typists, bookkeepers, and housekeepers. Together these people answer the phones, sort the mail, write the letters, buy supplies, collect the debts, and pay the bills.

Radio Station Owner. Radio stations in the United States are being bought and sold almost every day. Federal deregulation has made it relatively easy for anyone with adequate financing to purchase an AM or FM facility. It also is possible to build a radio station, providing you can find an available frequency, but the search may be slow, expensive, and open to competition from other applicants. It is advisable to have professional broadcast experience before undertaking the responsibilities of ownership. The radio spectrum is crowded with stations, many of which are not profitable. The most successful are operated by men and women who are up-to-date on broadcast technology, clever and sensitive programmers, experts at sales and promotions, and astute financial managers.

Radio General Manager/Station Manager. The general, or station, manager, selects, advises, and motivates department heads and supervisors to meet the station's financial goals and overall objectives. He or she provides strong leadership, especially in sales, and serves as sales manager in many small operations. Other duties include representing the station in dealings with governmental agencies and participating in broadcasting and local civic affairs. A college degree in communication, plus well-rounded experience in strategic marketing, programming, promotion, and public relations are necessary to be successful at this job. Average base salary: about $180,000. Some in major markets earn from $100,000 to $250,000.

Manager, Human Resources/Personnel Manager. This manager recruits and interviews job applicants, explains company policies and benefits to new employees, and responds to complaints and problems of employees. He or she prepares reports required by the Equal Employment Opportunity Commission (EEOC), the Occupational Safety and Health Administration (OSHA), and the Federal Communications Commission (FCC). The human resources manager also advises management on personnel matters. At small stations these duties may be handled by the manager, program director, or business manager. The position requires a college degree in personnel management or business administration, plus several years of experience in personnel work. The salary range is $20,000 to $40,000.

Business Manager/Controller. This person supervises the accounting department and is responsible for collecting and paying bills, issuing salary checks, assisting department heads in preparation of budgets, and compiling financial information and reports for management. He or she maintains the station's licenses, public inspection files, and official logs. In most locations the business manager also supervises the stockroom, telephone service, purchasing of supplies and equipment, and station security. Educational requirements are college training in business administration and accounting. Salaries vary with size of operation. The national average is about $47,000. Large market stations pay from $50,000 to $170,000.

TRAFFIC

The traffic department has been called the "paperwork heart" of a radio station. It is the repository and processing center for records of all commercial accounts, public service messages, programs, and features. Traffic prepares the daily broadcast schedule and provides performance reports for billing purposes. Most traffic departments are computerized operations.

Radio Traffic Manager/Supervisor. This employee prepares a minute-by-minute listing of all programs and commercials to be aired each day and maintains a record of the time that every segment was broadcast or omitted. This job requires business training, computer skills, and a methodical mind. Average small market salary is about $20,000. Large stations pay $25,000 to $35,000.

Radio Traffic Assistant. Where program and commercial activity is heavy, one or more traffic assistants may share the workload. In combined AM–FM operations, for example, AM traffic is handled by one person, FM by another. Computer and word-processor skills are necessary. Salary range is $15,000 to $20,000.

ENGINEERING

Every radio station must have at least one licensed chief engineer who is responsible for periodically inspecting, repairing, and maintaining the broadcast equipment. This person need not be a full-time employee but must work the number of hours necessary to fully perform the prescribed duties. Each station also is required to have a licensed operator on hand to monitor the transmitter during all hours of operation. Most stations now assign this responsibility to announcers and disc jockeys who have operator licenses.

With heavy automation and little need for a full-time engineer, many stations now employ a contract chief engineer to provide whatever inspections and services are required. Other technical duties are handled by licensed station personnel.

Full-time radio chief engineers have average earnings of $50,000, but larger AM and FM stations pay considerably more. Contract engineers charge about $12,000 annually to each station they serve, and they commonly work for more than one operation.

OFFICE SERVICE JOBS

A good way to get started in broadcasting is to find employment as a secretary, stenographer, receptionist, bookkeeper, or clerk-typist. Office assistants are in demand, but you should have a working knowledge of word processors, computers, fax machines, and duplicating equipment. Basic educational requirements are a high school diploma and some business school training or former employment in office services. With more education you may be able to advance to a better job. Salaries range from $15,000 to $25,000. The national average is about $19,000.

COMBO AND PART-TIME JOBS

Most radio stations in the United States and Canada have small staffs and depend on "combo" employees to do two or more different kinds of daily jobs. Your chances of getting hired for such work will pretty much depend on how skilled and versatile you are.

These are some typical combo positions: disk jockey/technician, announcer/newscaster, sportscaster/sales, receptionist/traffic, secretary/bookkeeper, reporter/newscaster/producer. Pay ranges from $15,000 to $25,000.

Some stations hire temporary help when needed and pay hourly wages but provide no company benefits. Quite a few AMs and FMs use part-time employees for less than forty hours a week to handle a specific shift or assignment. Amount of compensation varies according to the nature of the work and the experience of the employee.

NETWORK JOBS

Proliferation of radio networks that program for various demographic and ethnic audiences has improved employment prospects for talented programmers, talk-show hosts, producers, reporters, salespersons, technicians, and specialists in promotion, marketing, and affiliate relations.

CHAPTER 8

JOBS IN TELEVISION AND CABLE

In the expanding video universe almost every American household owns one or more television receivers. About 70 percent of TV homes are cable-connected, and a sizable number have modem attachments. Between 1997 and 1998, satellite subscribers jumped from three to six million. Computer hardware and software, VCRs, videotapes and disks bring sights, sounds, and interactive services into a multitude of homes, schools, businesses, and professions. This combined activity contributes to a healthy and growing job market.

A typical American commercial television station employs 93 people. You will find about 65 in the average small-market network affiliate and 27 at independent stations. In the twenty-five largest TV markets, staffs range from 115 to 150. Although the average cable TV system only has 12 employees, more than 500,000 people are estimated to be directly or indirectly dependent on cable for their livelihoods.

The entire television industry continues to be a bright spot in America's employment picture as institutions and individuals race to adopt advanced digital and computer technology and increase their usage of video devices for commercial and noncommercial purposes.*

---

*Sources: Cahners Research, *Broadcasting & Cable,* Jan. 12, 1998; National Cable Television Association Sourcebook, 1997.

OPPORTUNITY AND RESPONSIBILITY

The best-paying jobs in television are held by men and women who possess more than technical, programming, and production skills. They understand the interrelationship of media and see the potential in new forms of electronic communication. Most importantly, they are helping their employers capitalize on the rapid growth of interactive technology. NBC executive, Don Ohlmeyer, told the *New York Times* in January 1998, that the TV business had changed more in twenty-four months than in the previous twenty-four years. He predicted that "the companies that are going to succeed, must successfully reinvent themselves." For newcomers to the profession, this constitutes a bold challenge and a golden opportunity.

PROGRAM AND PRODUCTION JOBS

TV Program Manager/Director. Holder of this position sees that all local, network, and syndicated programming is broadcast as scheduled. Most stations formerly entrusted the program director with full responsibility for selecting and buying programs, but this has become such a costly and critical procedure, the task is now usually handled by a top-management committee that includes the program director and other department heads.

Some general managers or station managers handle major programming responsibilities, purchase films and TV shows, and decide when they are to be aired. In such cases the program director provides administrative assistance by supervising program personnel and working with the promotion, publicity, and research departments to market the station's programs and personalities. To qualify for a PD job you need a communications degree; creative and technical skills; and programming, personnel, and financial management experience. Salaries for program directors range from $27,000 to $75,000 or more. The national average is $54,000.

TV Community/Public Affairs Director. This job entails staying in touch with the public and developing programs, announcements, and special events to address matters of community interest or concern. Duties may include writing editorials, making speeches, and maintaining an FCC public inspection file. Applicants for this position should have a degree in communication; writing, speaking, and production skills; strong interest in community affairs; and several years of TV program or production experience. Pay ranges from $21,500 to $51,500. The national average is $45,000.

TV Production Manager. This department head coordinates and oversees all local production that originates in-house or at remote locations. Principal responsibility is hiring and supervising the work of producers, directors, floor managers, graphic artists, and production assistants. Duties also may include developing budgets, negotiating with talent, and working closely with technicians regarding video and audio needs. Job requirements are a communication or visual arts degree, knowledge of analog and digital technology, and several years of TV production experience. Salaries range from $30,000 to $58,000. Average national pay is $45,000.

TV Producer/Director. A producer/director develops and produces individual television programs or special events coverage. He or she discusses and approves budget, script, talent, sets, props, lighting, and sound. This person directs performers and technical crew in rehearsal and then produces, or "calls the shots," on the actual telecast. Most local TV productions are newscasts, interviews, and documentaries, so a producer should be well informed on current events and public affairs. Other job requirements are a liberal arts degree and experience as a production assistant. Salaries range from $24,000 to $53,000. The national average for all markets is about $33,000.

TV Production Assistant. This is an entry-level job that calls for providing any assistance needed by producers or directors. Duties may include doing word processing, researching, conducting preliminary interviews with newsmakers or talent, writing script or news copy, and running errands. A college degree helps in applying for this position. Some broadcast experience is also an advantage. Pay is modest, with the average starting salary at $17,000. Large market stations pay up to $25,000.

TV Copywriter/Producer. A copywriter/producer develops, writes, and produces commercial announcements and programs for local advertisers. He or she works closely with members of the sales staff in creating what clients want. This position is usually filled by a college graduate with training and experience in broadcasting, advertising, and production. The salary range is wide—$15,000 to $75,000.

TV Floor Director/Floor Manager. During the rehearsal and production of a television program, the floor director works in the studio alongside the performers and camera crew—giving cues, operating a prompter machine, overseeing set and prop changes, and relaying instructions from the producer in the control room. The position can be filled by a high school graduate, but a college graduate might consider this as a good place to get started in television. Pay ranges from $15,000 to $37,000. The average base salary is about $27,000.

Art Director/Graphic Artist. This person executes a variety of designs and illustrations for TV programs, newscasts, and station promotion. The work is done with electronic graphics equipment, commonly known as a character generator, Chyron, or Paint Box. This type of computer-artist is capable of creating titles, identifications, cartoons, portraits, landscapes, animation, and other visual concepts and ideas. Job requirements are an undergraduate art degree or training in commercial art, plus skills with computer software. Salary range is $25,000 to $60,000. Average national salary is $43,000.

Satellite Operations Manager/Tape-Film Manager. This manager is responsible for receiving, checking, filing, and returning tapes and films at a television station. Since nearly all news, advertising, and programming from outside sources is now delivered by satellite, other titles for this job are satellite operations manager or satellite traffic manager. The holder of this job books and coordinates satellite feeds and sees that they are routed correctly through the station's in-house and remote facilities. You must know how to operate satellite equipment in order to receive and transmit programming, and how to contract for satellite services in the United States, Canada, and abroad. Other job requirements are a high school education (minimum) or a college degree (preferred); technical broadcast training; and the ability to keep accurate logs and records. Salary range is $39,000 to $79,000. Average pay among all TV stations is $60,000.

TELEVISION PERSONALITIES

National Personalities. No one knows for sure why one person out of a million becomes a TV celebrity. Some say the biggest stars possess a mysterious, natural charisma. More likely they have gotten where they are by constantly working to improve their minds and perfect their talents. Perhaps luck played some part in helping performers like Jay Leno, Rosie O'Donnell, Bill Cosby, and Jane Pauley become rich and famous, but apparently the major factor was a driving determination to do their best.

Local Personalities. The best-liked local TV personalities are usually news anchors, sports anchors, weathercasters, and talk show hosts. Most small-town TV stations also have one or more popular and versatile staff members who are frequently seen reporting news, reading commercials, doing interviews, and covering other on-camera assignments.

A job like this, where available, would normally require that you have a college degree, have speech and broadcast training, and be well-read and able to talk intelligently on many subjects. It also helps to be neatly groomed and have a pleasing personality.

Some stations hire air personalities on a freelance, part-time, or contract basis and pay them $15,000 to $100,000 a year, or more. A general-assignment TV personality makes an average salary of $25,000 to $75,000.

MARKETING, PROMOTION, AND RESEARCH JOBS

TV Marketing Manager/Director. This marketing professional is responsible for developing strategic concepts and tailoring campaigns to increase the revenue, popularity, and prestige of a television station. The work entails initiating research projects and analyzing the results to determine unmet needs and wants of advertisers and viewers; then devising innovative ways to satisfy those needs by mobilizing the sales, programming, and promotional resources of the television station. This position is growing in importance. At some TV stations, the marketing director is next in authority to the manager. Pay ranges from $37,000 in a small station to $80,000 or more in a large one. The national average is about $70,000.

TV Promotion/Publicity Director. Often known as director of creative services, this person is responsible for promoting the television station's image, programs, and personalities through the use of advertising, publicity, promotion, and public relations. A major duty is producing in-house promotional spots with computer graphics. This department also prepares and distributes press releases, program schedules, promotional brochures, and pamphlets. It may also develop contests, special events, and public relations projects such as telethons, parades, and fund-raising dinners.

The job requires a college degree plus experience in one or more of these fields: broadcasting, advertising, public relations. Since media buying and other expenses are involved, knowledge of accounting and budgeting is an asset. Average base pay is about $50,000, but salaries range from $27,000 to $100,000, or more.

TV Promotion Assistant. A promotion assistant works under the supervision of the promotion director. The job demands creative promotional skills including mastery of electronic graphics. A promotion assistant helps develop various kinds of mass-media station-image promotional concepts.

Prerequisites are a degree in broadcasting or advertising and some TV experience. Average base pay for all markets is about $20,000 to $25,000.

TV Research Director. This person initiates and interprets research studies to help management make programming, sales, and marketing decisions. He or she knows how to collect and collate data through the use of electronic measuring devices and computers.

To prepare for this job, you need a college degree with knowledge of computerized research methodology, statistics, marketing, economics, and broadcasting.

Average salary is about $45,000. Small stations pay less. Large stations pay up to $75,000, or more. TV stations that do not have a research director contract for such services when needed or request assistance from the research departments of their national sales representatives.

SALES JOBS

Television selling is a complex and dynamic business that depends heavily on research, demographics, psychographics, and sophisticated marketing to satisfy the demands of advertisers. Unlike newspapers, magazines, and pay-TV, which collect subscriber fees, commercial television stations derive their revenue primarily from the sale of spot announcements and program sponsorships to local, regional, and national advertisers; and from allocation of certain time periods to networks, if they have such an affiliation. The amount and percentage of income derived from each source varies considerably. For example, national advertisers spend far more money in large markets than they do in small ones.

In addition to their own sales staffs, most television stations employ a national sales representative firm, with offices in principal cities, to reach and sell major advertisers throughout the country.

TV General Sales Manager. This person heads the television station's sales team. He or she has the responsibility for preparing sales forecasts and directs local and national sales efforts to meet budget projections in advertising sales.

Job requirements are a business or broadcasting degree; five years or more of television sales experience; and expertise in marketing, research, pricing, inventory control, finance, and personnel management. Average base pay is about $90,000, plus other compensation totaling $130,000. Large markets pay more.

TV National Sales Manager/Assistant Sales Manager. The national, or assistant, sales manager is responsible for selling and servicing of advertising accounts located beyond the TV station's primary coverage area. He or she works closely with national sales representatives and functions as assistant to the general sales manager in some operations.

Candidates should have a college degree; a minimum of three years in broadcast sales; and knowledge of marketing, research, and computers.

Compensation is likely to be salary plus a percentage of national advertising revenue. This total averages $100,000 annually; less in small markets, more in big ones.

TV Local Sales Manager. The local sales manager recruits, trains, and supervises a staff of local salespersons. He or she assigns accounts and checks reports of contacts made and results obtained. The job also entails working with the general sales manager and marketing and research directors to develop new kinds of business and increase the size of existing accounts.

Success as a salesperson and demonstrated management and marketing skills will help you to qualify for this job. You should have a college education and several years of impressive performance in sales and marketing.

Total pay may include commission on local sales. National average salary is about $70,000 a year. Total compensation is $100,000. The small market national average is $43,000 salary plus $8,000 additional compensation, totaling $51,000.

TV Account Executive/Salesperson. This job is involved with selling and marketing programs to local retail and corporate advertisers. An account executive must have good written and oral presentation skills, the ability to analyze and explain research findings and promote support services provided by the station, plus the ability to develop and retain accounts. Computer literacy and a college degree are preferred.

Annual compensation (salary plus commission) averages $60,000. Some go-getters make twice that much.

TV Sales Service Coordinator. This administrative assistant to the general sales manager collects, collates, and distributes TV sales information, manages sales data fed to and received from the computer, prepares sales research materials, and expedites trade agreements. The sales service coordinator also trains and supervises sales department assistants.

A college degree is preferred. Computer experience and a good record in business management are essential. Annual earnings average $45,000 salary plus $10,000 in other compensation.

TV Traffic Manager. The traffic manager is responsible for setting up and maintaining computerized scheduling instructions and timings for all commercial accounts, programs, and promotional and public service announcements. He or she assembles and processes data needed to produce the daily operational schedule.

The job requires computer skills, attention to detail, and accuracy. College training is desirable plus experience as a traffic assistant. Average salary is $37,000.

TV Sales/Traffic/Continuity Specialist. This employee checks content, length, and condition of commercial announcements, program materials, tapes, cassettes, and slides; oversees necessary corrections; and approves for broadcast. He or she also reviews and edits the daily program schedule before it is printed.

This position requires careful attention to detail and a methodical mind. A high school education is necessary, and broadcast experience is desirable. Salary range is $15,000 to $25,000.

TV Traffic/Computer Operator. He or she prepares a computer printout of the daily operational schedule and assists the traffic manager in maintaining a computerized inventory of the television station's advertising accounts and the time periods allocated to each one.

Job requirements are a high school education and expert computer skills. Average salary is $17,000.

TV Sales Order Processor. This person collects, verifies, and records on computer every advertising order received at the television station. He or she checks for accuracy and completeness of instructions. The sales order processor also may assist in preparation of sales and inventory reports.

Minimal job requirements are a high school diploma and computer skills. Business training and broadcast experience are helpful. Salary range is $15,000 to $25,000.

MANAGEMENT AND ADMINISTRATIVE JOBS

TV General Manager. Intense competition, changing technology, and rising costs have forced television mangers to become actively involved in the day-to-day operations of their stations. Together with department heads, the general manager makes decisions regarding programming, sales, hiring of personalities, and contracting for special events and promotions. Profit making has become so crucial that TV managers rely heavily on the advice of research, marketing, technical, and financial experts in making both short-term and long-term commitments.

To qualify for this position you should have a successful record of ten years or more in broadcast sales, programming, and management. Compensation may be a straight salary, or salary and bonus, based on station performance. National average earnings are $190,000.

TV Station Manager/Director of Broadcasting. Duties and responsibilities of this second-in-command position reflect the wishes of the general manager. Qualifications for the job are similar to those of the general manager, but compensation is less, averaging $105,000.

TV Operations Manager. Supervision of production and technical operations at the TV station is the daily responsibility of this official. The job requires technical and managerial capabilities. You should have a communication degree and considerable broadcast experience. Some TV news departments have their own operations managers. Salaries range from $45,000 to $85,000. The national average is $60,000.

Business Manager/Controller. This financial officer manages accounting policies and procedures; develops financial data for budgets, reports, and projections; supervises accounting employees; and serves as financial consultant to the general manager and all department heads. Duties may include purchase and maintenance of nontechnical equipment and supplies.

Position requires a business degree and accounting experience. Salary range is $35,000 to $90,000. The national average is $65,000.

TV Accountant/Bookkeeper. An accountant assists the business manager in running the financial operations of the television station. He or she handles accounts receivable and payable, billings, and payroll. The job also includes maintaining financial records for use by management in daily business dealings and budgeting. Prerequisites are business school training, knowledge of computers and other accounting machines, accuracy with figures, and an analytical mind.

The salary range is $20,000 to $40,000.

TV Manager of Human Resources. This person is responsible for recruiting job applicants and supplying department heads with names and resumes of prospective employees. The manager of human resources maintains records of all station employees and prepares required reports for management and the government. He or she communicates with employees regarding station guidelines, policies, and benefits and encourages activities to promote morale and job satisfaction.

College graduate preferred, with training and experience in personnel management. Average salary is about $49,000.

ENGINEERING JOBS

Most stations operate with fewer technicians than they did five years ago. Yet stations require more and different engineering expertise than ever before because of technological and marketplace changes.

Rapid and steady development of highly sophisticated communications equipment demands that technicians keep studying and learning about new devices and how best to use them. Expensive, intricate electronic components also require careful maintenance. Perhaps most importantly, engineering personnel are expected, as never before, to combine technical knowledge with a sharp sense of showmanship and a keen awareness of the need to be cost-conscious and budget-minded.

TV Chief Engineer. This department head manages a staff of technicians who operate, inspect, and maintain the studio cameras and microphones, projectors, remote-relay equipment, mobile telecasting units, videotape recorders, satellite receivers, transmitters, and antennae. The chief engineer prepares operating and capital budgets; advises management on communications research, development, and regulations; and recommends purchase of new electronic devices. The position requires knowledge of analog and digital video and audio technology, an engineering degree, a successful professional career, and the ability to manage efficiently and economically.

Average salary is about $65,000; the highest is $100,000 or more.

TV Technical Director. This specialist is responsible for the technical quality of a television production and supervises the technical crew. The technical director transmits instructions from the producer to camera operators and sound and lighting technicians. The job also involves operating video switching equipment. It requires a combination of technical know-how and creative production talents. Salary range is $21,000 to $37,000. The average for all markets is $29,000.

Technicians

The average commercial television station employs about nine operator technicians and four maintenance technicians. Operator technicians earn $20,000 to $40,000 a year. Maintenance technicians make $25,000 to $45,000. Prerequisites for employment are a high school diploma, technical training, prior experience at a radio station or smaller TV station, and an aptitude for being either an operations or a maintenance specialist. These are typical TV technician jobs:

TV Audio Operator. The audio operator is responsible for the audio portion of a television program, controls switching of microphones, and monitors sound levels on voices, music, and special effects.

TV Video Operator. The video operator is responsible for the television picture, performs the necessary functions to control brightness and color levels, and monitors transmission of the video signal to the transmitter.

Camera Operator/Videographer. This person operates both full-sized studio cameras and smaller ENG (electronic news gathering) cameras inside a studio or on location, and focuses on the action as directed by the producer/director. Some TV stations and network news programs have replaced camera operators with computer-controlled robotic cameras.

Videotape/Film Operator. This person is responsible for operating the recording, playback, and editing functions at a TV station. He or she cues up and projects tapes, films, cassettes, or slides, as scheduled or called for by the producer/director.

TV Maintenance Technician. Maintenance technicians are responsible for repair and servicing of a TV station's communications equipment and facilities. Each technician usually is assigned one area of maintenance responsibility, such as transmitter, ENG cameras, studio cameras and switchers, satellite facilities, or automotive and aircraft communication devices.

NETWORK TELEVISION JOBS

TV network jobs are similar in most respects to those found at a television station. People work in programming, sales, news, engineering, promotion, public relations, research, human resources, and general administration. In addition, networks have legal and affiliate-relations departments. When hiring performers, networks tend to prefer persons with considerable experience and impressive credentials. Openings are often filled by promoting individuals already on the payroll. Some network salaries—especially those of news anchors—are high, but compensation for most positions is about the same as at large TV stations. Employment prospects at TV networks are improving as they invest in cable and Internet operations.

CABLE TV EMPLOYMENT

From modest beginnings in rural America, cable television now comprises thousands of separate systems that blanket the country and provide job opportunities in sales, programming, production, research, and distribution. Cable subscribers pay a basic monthly fee to receive various channels of TV programs. Extra charges are levied for channels that feature recent movies, special events, and commercial services.

Most cable systems solicit advertising. A growing number produce and sell local programs and commercials. Each system sets aside one or more public access channels where organizations or individuals are permitted to present their views and demonstrate their talents.

Cable programming—combined with new service offerings such as high speed access to the Internet—makes cable one of the nation's most popular and fastest-growing purveyors of entertainment, information, and education.

Robert Alter, National Cable Television Association executive, encourages students to learn more about cable. "The outlook for the future is very promising," he says. "So I feel quite comfortable in urging young people to make a career in the cable industry."

Positions in cable TV include the following:

General Manager/System Manager. As head of a cable system, this executive hires, directs, and consults with department heads and oversees the entire cable system operation. Qualifications require a communications degree, broadcast/cable experience, and both technical and management expertise. Pay varies according to the size of cable systems. The range is $60,000 to $275,000.

Chief Engineer. Holder of this position manages a team of skilled technicians who install, operate, and maintain all of the cable system's telecasting equipment. This position requires an engineering degree, considerable broadcast experience, and technical, financial, and management expertise. Salaries range from $45,000 in small systems to $75,000 in large ones.

Technical Operations Manager. This electronic expert supervises the cable system's technical staff. The position requires a high degree of cable know-how and broadcasting experience. Management skills also are important. Annual salaries range from $45,000 to $75,000.

Technician. This job title covers a number of different kinds of work involved in installing, operating, repairing, and servicing cable system facilities. Some technicians fix damaged cable, amplifiers, or converter boxes. Others correct malfunctions in subscribers' equipment. Installers connect homes and businesses to the cable system. Technical schooling and experience are prerequisites. Pay averages $20,000 to $40,000.

Marketing Manager. This executive oversees all of the cable system's marketing, promotion, publicity, advertising, and direct sales to subscribers. To qualify, you need a college degree in communication plus sales and marketing experience. Compensation goes from $35,000 in small systems to $90,000 in large ones.

Programming Manager. The position involves selecting, scheduling, and sometimes developing programs and features for airing on various cable channels. This executive also supervises program department assistants. Broadcast programming experience and research capabilities help in qualifying for this job. Salaries run from $30,000 to $60,000.

Program/Production Assistant. Holder of this job assists the program manager and may be assigned writing, directing, and promotion duties. The job pays $18,000 to $20,000.

Producer/Director. This department head produces and directs programs created by the cable system. Sometimes referred to as director of local originations, the position requires a college degree in communication or theatrical arts and several years of broadcast cable experience. Salaries average $20,000 to $40,000.

Advertising/Sales Manager. This executive directs the cable system's sales staff and leads their efforts to add more subscribers and advertisers. College courses in marketing and professional experience in sales and advertising are assets in first obtaining a cable sales position and then advancing to the management level, where salaries run from $35,000 to more than $50,000.

Account Executive/Salesperson. If hired for this job, you may recruit cable system subscribers or sell cable advertising. Cable systems sometimes hire advertising majors and specialists in telemarketing, sales to hotel intranet systems, and pay-per-view customers. Compensation—salary plus commission—averages $20,000 to $40,000 in small cable systems and $25,000 to $100,000 in large systems.

Customer Service Manager. This department manager recruits and supervises a staff of customer representatives, who respond to requests and complaints from cable subscribers. The job requires education and experience in cable operations, human relations, and business management. The job pays $30,000 to $50,000 annually.

Customer Service Representative. This employee deals directly with cable customers, by phone or in person, and tries to resolve problems and keep cable subscribers satisfied. College training in public relations and knowledge of cable system policies and programming are helpful in qualifying for this job. Pay ranges from $15,000 to $30,000.

Director of Public Access. This job entails managing one or more public access channels and making free time available to the public for broadcast of noncommercial programs. Participants are assisted in use of production facilities. The position requires a communication degree and broadcast experience. Interest in social services is helpful. Pay runs from $15,000 to $30,000 a year.

Public Access Coordinator. Holder of this job works for the director of public access, scheduling usage of cable access facilities and providing participants with information, advice, and production assistance. Duties may be performed inside a studio or at remote locations. Prerequisites are TV program and production experience, patience, and teacher talents. The salary range is $12,500 to $25,000.

CHAPTER 9

ELECTRONIC NEWS CAREERS

There will always be employment opportunities for earnest, competent, electronic journalists. They are needed to satisfy the public's insatiable appetite for news. But John Dancy, veteran of more than thirty years with NBC News, is concerned that too many newcomers to the profession try to be entertainers rather than serious and responsible reporters of facts and information.

Many aren't properly trained and lack news judgment. Some can't even read or write coherently and therefore are unable to convey the substance of news stories to the public.

Dancy advises beginners to start at a smaller-market radio or television station, where they will have ample opportunities to learn how to investigate, interview, write, edit, and report all kinds of news.*

Foreign locations, in Dancy's opinion, are also good places for adventurous young journalists to gain experience in evaluating news happenings and communicating their significance.

Mastering the art and technology of electronic journalism will make you better qualified and improve your chances of finding the type of broadcast news job you want.

TELEVISION NEWS

The average television station employs thirty-five to forty news personnel and devotes most of its local program time to news, sports, weather reports, and hometown interviews and features. News staffs of fifty or more are com-

---

*Source: William Kirtz, "Dancy Laments TV News Today," *Quill,* Society of Professional Journalists, Jan./Feb. 1997.

mon in large city TV operations. Although they might earn more doing something else, thousands of young men and women choose to be television journalists. Professor Vernon A. Stone of the University of Missouri calls it "Love of the job rather than a desire to make money."

Competition for TV news jobs is keen, and technical competence is stressed as a necessary qualification. Digital equipment is widely used for writing and editing copy and video footage. Reporters carry ENG cameras and report from virtually any location by microwave or satellite. Versatility is a major consideration in hiring people for news jobs. Applicants are judged on their ability to track down news stories and to write, edit, and report them on the air. The trend is toward selecting aggressive, reliant, and personable electronic newspeople.

News producers, directors, and editors are having to acquire more technical knowledge, as news room operations make greater use of time-saving technology. And news management is paying close attention to research, budgeting, and cost-cutting measures.

As for the news product, Richard Mallory, vice president for news, Gannett Broadcasting, foresees television stations steadily increasing their output of news to compete with cable's twenty-four-hour worldwide news service. Many TV stations now offer round-the-clock news coverage over the air and on the Internet, with heavy emphasis on hard local news.

Here are some of the most sought-after TV news jobs:

TV News Director. This department head manages a staff of news anchors, reporters, editors, producers, camera operators, technicians, and assistants. The position requires a communications degree, at least five years of reporting and evaluating news, plus leadership skills and expertise in administrative, financial, and personnel management. Salaries range from $34,500 to $127,000. The national average is $83,000.

TV Assistant News Director/Assignment Editor. This person is second in command in the news department. He or she supervises the news room staff, makes assignments, solves problems as they arise, and assists the news director in budgeting and long-range planning.

Job requirements are a journalism or broadcasting degree, at least three years of TV news experience, and management potential. Salary range is $28,000 to $45,000. Average pay for all markets is $34,000.

TV News Producer/Director. The producer/director is responsible for planning, preparation, and production of television newscasts. This is a graphics-intensive, complex process that requires a clear, cool head, imaginative showmanship, and sound news judgment.

Prerequisites are a college degree in broadcasting or journalism plus experience in writing, reporting, and editing news. Salary range is $25,000 to $50,000. Average pay nationally is $32,000.

TV News Production Assistant. Duties of this job vary according to the needs of the senior producer but may include checking out news tips, writing and rewriting news, editing and timing news tapes, and assembling segments of a newscast.

A college degree and previous broadcast news experience are required. Starting salary is about $17,000. Average pay for all markets is $20,000.

TV News Reporter. A TV news reporter covers local news, everything from fires and murders to meetings with the mayor and civic club luncheons.

The job requires knowing how to interview and how to interpret many kinds of information. The ability to write and speak well and proficiency in use of cameras, recorders, and electronic transmission devices are also essential. To qualify you should have a degree in electronic communication. Salaries range from $18,000 for beginners to $50,000 or more for experienced reporters.

TV News Anchor. This person is the foremost personality around whom a major TV newscast is built. The news anchor reads news items and introduces live and taped inserts by other reporters and correspondents. This coveted position pays well but demands proven skills as a news communicator. Duties may include investigative reporting; interviewing; writing news; editing copy and videotape; hosting discussions, debates, and documentaries; making speeches and personal appearances; and participating in TV station promotion and public service campaigns.

Job requirements are a college degree, several years of TV news experience, typing and computer knowledge, and the ability to look and sound pleasant and authoritative. Average annual compensation is $73,000, but pay in larger markets exceeds $100,000. Some senior anchors make $250,000 to $1,000,000.

TV News Photographer/Cameraperson. A news photographer covers news live with an (ENG) electronic news-gathering camera or uses a camcorder to tape reports. In addition to photographic responsibilities, duties may include writing and reporting news stories and editing tapes.

Qualifications required are a high school diploma plus previous photographic or television news experience. Average annual compensation is $28,000.

TV Sports Director/Sports Anchor. This person is responsible for sports news and play-by-play coverage presented by a television station. He or she may be required to carry a camera and shoot interviews or sports events live or on tape.

Job requirements are a college degree, knowledge of sports, and the ability to communicate with accuracy and authority. Typical salary is $54,000. Some stations pay $75,000 and higher.

TV Weather Anchor/Meteorologist. He or she collects, analyzes, and reports weather information. Added importance is attached to the position when the forecaster is a certified meteorologist.

National average salary is $55,000, but some earn twice that much.

TV Newswriter. This job exists mainly at networks and stations that present news twenty-four hours a day. Responsibilities are primarily to write, edit, and rewrite news stories, based on information supplied by reporters, correspondents, and wire services. Resulting copy is used on newscasts, documentaries, and news specials.

Job requirements are a journalism/broadcast degree and superior newswriting skills. Salary range is $15,000 to $30,000.

TV News Graphics Artist. This person creates the lettering, designs, identifications, graphs, cartoons, and other visual effects that serve to illustrate and add pictorial interest to a news presentation.

The job requires news know-how, computer graphics skills, and creative artistry. Salary range is $20,000 to $45,000.

TV News Archivist/Librarian. Holder of this job is responsible for indexing and filing news tapes and films, maintaining a computerized inventory of every sound bite, prominent person, and important news event in the station's archives, so that material can be quickly recalled when needed. May also edit and repair tapes and act as custodian of news cameras and related video equipment.

A high school diploma is required; technical training is helpful. The job also demands experience in the operation of recording and editing machines and other audiovisual equipment. Salary range is $12,000 to $25,000.

TV News Technician/Video Coordinator. This job exists in busy news operations that require their own technicians. Major areas of responsibility are operation and maintenance of microwave, satellite, and electronic newsgathering equipment. Duties may involve inside and outside assignments.

The job requires technical training or a degree plus several years experience in radio or TV engineering. Salary range is $25,000 to $40,000.

TV Airborne Reporter. This job entails spotting and reporting traffic problems and covering news stories from an airplane or helicopter. Usually the reporter is also a licensed pilot and flies the aircraft.

In addition to news training and experience, this reporter can benefit from being a versatile performer and storyteller. Annual compensation ranges from $30,000 to $100,000.

TV News Assistant. This entry-level position enables a beginner to learn what television news is all about. Duties may include answering phones, keeping news machines stocked with paper and ribbons, filing news scripts, and doing general secretarial chores. Promotion to a higher paying job depends on demonstrated dependability and proficiency.

A high school diploma is acceptable, but college training is preferred. News assistants should have typing and word-processing skills. Many TV news departments hire student interns for this job. Pay for beginners is modest, averaging about $200 to $250 a week. Experienced assistants make $15,000 to $20,000 a year.

TV News Specialist. Television has cultivated a number of news and information jobs, each of which calls for extensive knowledge of a particular subject. Newscasts commonly feature experts on consumer affairs, financial management, personal health, urban problems, environmental science, politics, and military affairs. Some specialists are full-time staff employees, but many freelance and work when needed on a contract basis. TV news specialists generally have achieved professional success and recognition as authorities in their field of work. They also have good communication skills.

Salaries for full-time positions range from $25,000 to $100,000. Contract employees at local stations average $50 to $150 per appearance.

Weekend TV News Jobs. As an economy measure, many TV news operations hire people to work weekends only as news anchors, reporters, videographers, and producers. Since this is part-time employment, it is possible to fill such a position and hold another job elsewhere. Educational and professional qualifications are the same as for full-time employees. The pay range is about $100 a day.

Median TV News Salaries (By Region)

Region	News Director	Producer	Anchor	Reporter	Photographer
Northeast	$65,000	$25,000	$41,000	$25,000	$27,000
South	50,000	22,000	40,000	20,000	20,000
Midwest	50,000	22,000	42,000	22,000	19,000
West	54,000	26,000	39,000	26,000	22,000

Source: Radio and Television News Directors Association/Ball State University survey, reported in *RTNDA Communicator*, March 1997.

RADIO NEWS

Nine out of ten radio stations claim to have news departments, but the majority are staffed by only one full-time employee. The remaining news duties are handled by part-timers or announcers, who double as newscasters. Radio stations that are news-active have an average of five employees—the news director, two reporters, and two news announcers.

Salary levels in radio news remain low. Still, radio news continues to attract young men and women because it goes where the action is, relaying to the public live reports of what is happening locally and around the world. There are some 700 all-news operations in the country, and several thousand others use radio cars, helicopters, and airplanes to cover local news, traffic, and special events. Since this type of journalism combines speed, simplicity, and availability to mobile listeners, as well as those in homes and workplaces, radio news will continue to be an important broadcast service and a good training ground for news-minded young people.

Radio News Director. This job requires a good journalism-broadcasting education, several years of news writing and reporting, plus management capabilities. Where a radio news staff is small—and most are—the news director may do much of the reporting, editing, newscasting, monitoring of news machines and police and fire signals, and response to phone tips and inquiries.

The average salary of radio news directors nationwide is about $44,000. In major markets they average $56,000, with some stations paying as high as $75,000, according to industry surveys.

Radio News Reporter. This job provides the kind of experience needed to become a news director or news anchor. The daily, active routine involves checking out news tips, interviewing news sources, writing and editing news copy, and reporting live or on tape. Equipment used includes tape recorders, shortwave radio, cellular phone, microwave, radio cars, and sometimes aircraft. Reporters at most radio stations also deliver newscasts. The national average salary for radio reporters is $35,000.

Radio News Anchor/High Anchor. The job requires preparing and delivering newscasts from wire copy, local stories, and live and taped reports. Because of limited personnel, anchors commonly do reporting, writing, editing, and other airwork, in addition to their newscasts. High anchors are likely to do only featured newscasts and get more assistance in their preparation. They also receive more publicity and make more money.

Although radio anchors need considerable education and experience, they average earnings of $34,000 nationwide. Large news operations pay anchors

$25,000 to $60,000. Salaries for high anchors range from $30,000 to $150,000.

Radio Sports Director. The holder of this position has responsibility for coverage of sports news and athletic events, including live play-by-play, interviews, and taped reports. National average salary is $46,000. Popular and experienced sports reporters may earn $50,000 to $100,000, or more.

Radio News Editor/Writer. This job exists primarily in all-news stations, news services, and news networks. Most radio stations expect reporters and anchors to do their own writing and editing. Prerequisites are a college degree in journalism or broadcasting and proven ability at news writing and editing. National average salary range for this position, where available, is $20,000 to $30,000.

Radio Traffic Reporter. Some stations employ one or more reporters to keep a watch on traffic conditions and make periodic reports, particularly during morning and afternoon rush hours. Surveillance is maintained from a helicopter, airplane, or automobile. Traffic reporters frequently spot and cover news events, such as collisions, fires, and holdups. Prerequisites are a college education, news experience, and a pilot's license, where aircraft are used. Salary range is $23,000 to $50,000.

Median Radio News Salaries (By Market Size)

Position	*Major Market*	*Large Market*	*Middle Market*	*Small Market*
News Director	$36,500	$27,000	$22,000	$21,000
News Producer	24,000	30,000	20,000	22,000
News Anchor	26,000	21,500	20,000	13,000
News Reporter	35,000	23,000	18,000	18,000

Source: Radio and Television News Directors Association/Ball State University survey, reported in *RTNDA Communicator*, March 1997.

RADIO NEWS OUTSOURCING

Radio news jobs are moving from inside the station to other locations. Hundreds of news departments are being downsized or eliminated and replaced by outside news sources. Metro Network News Service, for example, feeds newscasts and traffic reports to more than 250 AMs and FMs in 35 markets. Shadow Broadcasting, with a staff of fifty reporters and editors, serves

23 radio outlets in Houston, Texas, plus 110 more in 14 other markets. The Weather Network transmits periodic reports to facilities coast to coast. News services like this have frequent openings for reporters, newscasters, and weathercasters.

Jobs also can be found at 23 state radio networks where senior reporters make $25,000 to $44,000 and regular reporters and anchors average $20,000 to $25,000.

As broadcasters enhance their audio-video capabilities with digital technology and establish outposts on cable and the Internet, they will develop and market many kinds of news and information. This should increase employment opportunities for radio and TV journalists. More jobs also are likely to be created by radio stations that resume intensive coverage of local news and community affairs in order to compete with other formats.

CABLE NEWS

Cable news networks are leading the world into a new era of immediate electronic journalism populated by dozens of national, regional, and local cable news services. Whereas viewers used to watch one or two TV newscasts a day at specified times, millions now turn to an all-news channel and catch up on what's happening at any moment, day or night. Traditional network news departments have responded to this threat to their dominance by creating competing twenty-four-hour cable news operations.

Cable news rivals have become more innovative and their reporting more diversified as they attempt to attract and hold audiences for long periods each day, rather than just when a big news event occurs.

"There are different ways to address issues at different times of the day," says Gail Evans, executive vice president of CNN, which serves viewers around the clock in 210 countries. NBC, CBS, ABC, and Fox are responding by increasing the quantity and variety of their long- and short-form cable news.

The growing popularity of cable news has spawned scores of specialized news services and created numerous jobs, especially for authorities on various subjects, such as medicine, music, military affairs, law, economics, government, environmental science, entertainment, sports, and the weather.

A promising number of news jobs also are being created by TV stations, newspapers, and other media that use cable channels to expand their coverage and promote their services. Your prospects for cable news employment will be enhanced if you can suggest interesting new ways to report pertinent information. As news departments make the transition from analog to digital systems, their high-quality visual and aural presentations will stimulate even more electronic news employment.

A word of caution though: Many cable news sources stress immediacy and sensationalism. This type of "now" journalism—fragmented, disjointed, often without context—is sometimes of questionable news value and appears to be mainly "infotainment." You should avoid any tempting offers to engage in this kind of reporting and look for a position with a cable operation that deals in reputable journalism.

Cable Network News Salaries

POSITIONS	LOW	AVERAGE	HIGH
Reporter	$45–55,000	$65–85,000	$80–200,000
Assignment Editor	30–50,000	50–70,000	70–90,000
Producer	40–50,000	40–70,000	70–90,000
Videotape Editor	40–50,000	40–70,000	70–120,000
Cameraperson	25–40,000	40–60,000	60–100,000
Writers	30–40,000	45–55,000	55–65,000
Video Journalist/Apprentice	15–20,000		
Correspondents*	90–100,000	100–120,000	120–200,000

*Some cable anchors and correspondents, who are famous and popular, command annual salaries ranging from $800,000 upward to a million or more.

Source: Data obtained from representatives of various cable news networks; 1998 salaries vary according to size of the cable news operation.

MULTIMEDIA JOURNALISTS

Help-wanted ads for news professionals repeatedly emphasize that applicants must have a working knowledge of computers, satellites, and digital technology. Electronic journalists are now using machines and devices that combine the capabilities of TV, radio, cable, print, and other media. News departments are acquiring digital cameras, recorders, and graphic design and editing equipment. In addition to writing, speaking, and investigative skills, future TV and radio reporters will need to be technically trained multimedia communicators.

Electronic News Careers 99

BUSINESS NEWS JOBS

The stock market is attracting millions of new investors, and the public generally is keenly interested in receiving periodic reports from Wall Street and foreign markets, as well as other pertinent financial information. Business news has become a regular daily feature on TV, radio, cable, and the Internet. Several cable networks report financial news around the clock, including continual updates on the value of various stocks, bonds, and currencies.

Numerous local and network programs feature discussion and analysis of what's happening in commerce, industry, and the world's money markets. Since business news has become such a popular topic, demand has increased for financial news reporters. You should have a degree in commerce and news reporting experience to qualify for this position. Pay ranges from $25,000 to $75,000 and up.

ELECTRONIC TABLOIDS

Numerous network and syndicated programs concentrate on news and commentary about personalities and celebrities. Much of what is reported comes from unnamed sources, often borders on the sensational or sordid, and may or may not be true. But the public appears to be fascinated with intimate gossip about famous and infamous entertainers, musicians, politicians, athletes, and other well-known and photogenic figures. Jobs are available for investigative reporters and photographers, but you should take care to work only for a reputable organization. Pay is generally good if you are productive.

GLOBAL NEWS JOBS

Expanding satellite-delivery news services are creating some jobs for journalists who are proficient in more than one language and willing to work in a foreign country. Organizations involved in international news competition include WTN-Worldwide Television News, APTV-Associated Press Television News Service, and Reuters TV.

WTN provides clients in Europe, Asia, North America, and South America with twenty-four-hour news, sports, and entertainment reports. Broadcast subscribers in the United States receive hourly newscasts plus frequent feeds on breaking news events.

APTV serves more than 130 print and broadcast clients throughout the world and maintains news bureaus in New York, Los Angeles, Washington, and Miami.

Reuters TV delivers news twenty-four hours a day by satellite to more than 900 broadcasters all over the globe. It also supplies financial news via computer to more than 14,000 traders and analysts.

NBC, ABC, CBS, and other networks also maintain news bureaus in foreign countries and staff them with bilingual correspondents.

NEWSPAPER WEBSITES

In virtually all large United States cities, daily newspapers maintain twenty-four-hour websites that provide access to a host of news and information sources and encourage interactive participation by computer users. Each website is staffed by editors, reporters, researchers, and technical personnel.

A typical news website combines newspaper, radio, and television techniques and supplies breaking news stories as well as updated coverage of major happenings, commentaries, features, and periodic reports on financial matters, sports, politics, entertainment, and other subjects.

SPORTSCASTING

Sportscasting differs from most other broadcasting jobs in working conditions and compensation. "It's very subjective, much like picking movie actors and actresses," explains Cathy Griffin, a sports marketing veteran. Numerous anonymous or little-known sports reporters earn modest hourly wages. Play-by-play announcers are better paid. A fortunate few have distinctive voices, "translate well on camera, and light up the TV screen." These charismatic personalities are usually well informed about sports, speak authoritatively, and command high salaries.

John Madden, NFL commentator, is reputed to make more than $4 million a year. Keith Olbermann turned down a $700,000 contract with ESPN in Connecticut and signed for $600,000 with MSNBC because he prefers working in Manhattan.

Harry Carey, legendary Chicago sportscaster, made an estimated million dollars a year. His son, Skip, is reported to receive nearly that much from the Atlanta Braves. And his grandson, Chip, is believed to earn a similar amount with the Chicago Cubs.

Sportcasting is a demanding profession, requiring that you know the history and rules of various sports and be able to quickly recall interesting and pertinent facts about athletes and memorable sporting events. You must be prepared to travel, keep abreast of what's happening in sports, be a competent interviewer, and possess colorful, accurate announcing skills.

Pay for local TV, radio, and cable sportscasters ranges from $20,000 in smaller markets to $150,000 or more in major markets.

CAREER ADVICE FROM NEWS EXPERTS

Q. What is the reporter's role in society?

A. Sam Donaldson, ABC: "I always thought the reporter's role was to find out what was happening and report that to an audience. That role continues. But how we find out what is happening and how we report it is changing rapidly. Technology is one thing. News can now be broadcast instantly worldwide. And getting a story requires greater sophistication and understanding and research. But the basic function of a reporter—to find out what is going on in the laboratory, in the workplace, in the political forum—has not changed. Good journalism survives if journalists have the wit to adapt to changing times."

Q. Has the reporter's role changed since you became a network news anchor in 1962?

A. Walter Cronkite, legendary CBS newsman: "It's changed in a couple of ways. One, because our news personalities are more personally known now, so that has changed the perception of the news considerably. It's become far more personal than it was before. Also in some ways the responsibility of the press is greater, particularly in our presidential politics, but to a degree in other politics as well. Also, consumer journalism has become a major part of journalistic responsibility, which it never was before. I mean talking about products and their efficiency or their failure. And that's cast a new light on journalistic responsibility, which I think is fine."

Q. What lessons have you learned about the art of interviewing?

A. Mike Wallace, CBS: "The importance of research and the importance of listening. By the time you've written several dozen questions, you've done enough research so that you have a fair understanding of almost anything that comes up."

Q. Is new technology affecting the broadcasting of news?

A. Hugh Downs, ABC: "It has particularly affected the speed with which we can get something on the air; some of the ways we present material to make sure the audience is with us. I think that is for the better, but there is a downside. I think the public suffers from information overload. But on balance I would say it's an asset."

Q. How do you think news will be reported in the next ten years?

A. Tim Russert, NBC: "It will continue to be rapid and simultaneous in any breaking crisis. It will continue to expand. I believe there will be more and more narrowcasting as people have access to hundreds of cable stations and satellite dishes. And the Internet will continue to thrive."

Q. Do you recommend continuing education for a newsperson?

A. Bettina Luscher, CNN, Germany: "I am still profiting from the two years I spent studying politics at the University of Wisconsin in Madison; an opportunity granted to me by a scholarship from the Fulbright Foundation. The scholarship gave me more insight into America and taught me always to look at something from various points of view, to get the news across so that it is understandable for every country in the world."

Q. What changes in news reporting have you experienced?

A. Rita Braver, CBS chief White House correspondent: "Advances in technology from film to videotape, and from hardline to satellite make it quicker and easier to get news on the air than any of us ever dreamed would be possible. And that means the burden is increasing to be careful, to try to put a story into context, to try to convey to the public that we don't 'know it all,' but are just trying to give the best picture of what is going on at the time."

CHAPTER 10

INTERNET BROADCASTING

The combining of once-separate technologies has created a gigantic new form of electronic communication—the Internet. This global network embodies some characteristics of print journalism, television, radio, and telephone. Yet it is a uniquely different digital, interactive concept. L. Robert Gould, President of Web Sine, Inc., calls it "Internet Broadcast." Kenneth E. Mueller of the Museum of Television and Radio considers Internet audio to be a form of radio with a different delivery system. Vince Giuliano, who conducts an electronic community forum each week on the *New York Times* website envisions the Internet as a revolutionary new medium for erasing communication barriers and distances.

This newcomer to the broadcasting-narrowcasting family consists of a worldwide computer network, thousands of websites, and millions of surfers. Almost every major company in the United States and Canada, including two-thirds of the Fortune-500, have websites, and more are coming on-line daily. Consumer buying on the Internet topped $2.5 billion in 1997, and classified ad revenue totaled $125 million. Forrester Research expects annual Internet sales to exceed $17 billion by 2006.

Computer users are steadily increasing and spending more time cruising in cyberspace. They averaged 12.8 hours per week in 1997. Intensified interest in the Internet has been a boon to employment agencies. College placement offices report repeated requests for computer science and information technology graduates. Mordy Levine of Hall Kinion & Associates, a California recruiting firm, believes that further Internet growth is inevitable. "Don't mistakenly think that everything grinds to a halt five years into the millennium," he says. "There is an incredible demand for skills related to the Internet."*

---

*Sources: *Business Week,* May 11, 1997; *New York Times,* May 6, 1997; *Atlanta Journal-Constitution,* May 11, 1997; Georgia Tech Research Corp./GVU Center.

INTERNET EMPLOYMENT

Jobs spawned by the Internet are plentiful and increasing as companies contract with developers to create websites, which they then use to promote and market their products and services. Specialists in designing, programming, and managing websites are making excellent salaries.

These are some of the jobs commonly found on an Internet site development team, together with estimated salaries:

Position	Small Market	Large Market
General Manager	$60,000	$95,000
Advertising Manager	45,000	70,000
Technical Director	50,000	80,000
Marketing Manager	50,000	70,000
Content/Program Manager	50,000	70,000
Account Executive	25,000	40,000
Programmer/Web Master	45,000	65,000
Senior Producer/Editor	35,000	60,000
Content Producer/Developer	25,000	35,000
Art Director	45,000	70,000
Graphics Designer	25,000	35,000
Multimedia Developer	25,000	35,000
Classified Manager	30,000	45,000

Source: Salaries are averages based on information obtained from numerous website development agencies.

Corporate Website Jobs*

Rapid growth of corporate websites and increased emphasis on Internet and Intranet communication by industries, retailers, wholesalers, and service businesses has created a sizable number of new jobs. The average corporate website is operated by fourteen people. Many others range in size from one to several hundred employees.

These are some typical website job titles and salaries:

Position	Salary
Vice President/General Manager	$110,000
On-line Licensing Manager	100,000
Director of On-line Sales and Marketing	95,000
Web Manager/Administration	64,000

Position	Salary
On-line Sales/Account Executive	62,500
On-line Product Manager	61,000
Audio Engineer	60,000
Videographer	58,000
Content Manager	52,500
Web Programmer	49,000
Resident On-line Analyst	46,000
Web Artist/Layout Editor	46,000
Data Control Technician	41,500

Some companies augment salaries with annual bonuses. For more information about corporate website jobs, check newspapers and technical magazines, inquire at computer training schools, and contact employment agencies that recruit website professionals. Numerous job openings also are listed at various locations on the Internet.

*Source: National survey of corporate website jobs, conducted by Buck Consultants, Stamford, Connecticut 1997.

Internet News Jobs

TV and radio networks, newspapers, magazines, phone companies, and makers of software have all been active and aggressive in establishing Internet news operations. Some of the major participants include NBC, CBS, ABC, CNN, Fox, MCI, Conus, Bloomberg, Cox, the Hearst Corporation, and virtually all of the country's large newspapers and magazines.

Major daily newspapers in the top fifty markets maintain websites and make their informational resources available to Internet consumers and advertisers. Their Internet operations resemble both print and broadcast news departments. Staffs of editorial and technical professionals, largely recruited from TV stations and newspapers, prepare and transmit audio, video, and printed news reports, interviews, discussions, interactive features, and advertising. Each website markets an array of distinctive, personalized information services.

The Microsoft Corporation and CNBC employ several hundred journalists at their combined website and twenty-four-hour news-and-talk cable network. C-NET, a company that specializes in news about information technology, has a website staff of twenty-five. Reporters and researchers start at about $25,000. Senior editors earn as much as $80,000.

Internet news services usually charge a fee for providing specific information. Sometimes referred to as "utilitarian journalism," computerized reference sources are expected to grow into a multibillion dollar industry. This should result in more jobs for specialists in news, advertising, sales, research, and digital technology. News professionals now employed on the Internet include: editors, reporters, producers, graphic artists, newscasters, sportscasters, researchers, archivists, and advertising solicitors. Pay for these positions is comparable to salaries in newspapers and TV stations.

Computer Systems Jobs

Certified Professional. Holder of this certification has been trained, examined, and judged qualified to design, install, operate, and troubleshoot computer software systems. Starting salaries range from $35,000 to $40,000. A technical software specialist with five or more years of experience may earn $50,000 to $60,000, or more.

Certified Systems/Network Engineer. This position requires training and experience in setting up and overseeing the operation of interactive computer systems and networks. Known also as a netware engineer, the job usually requires a minimum of one to five years experience. Pay averages $70,000 to $80,000.

Certified Internet Specialist. This software web master is qualified by training and experience to create websites and is a certified professional in the design, organization, and operation of both local-area and wide-area computer systems. Salaries vary from $35,000 to more than $75,000, depending on experience and performance record. A 1997 survey by *Microsoft Certified Professional Magazine* reported an annual average salary of $57,300 for a software product specialist.

Certified Technician. This specialist is concerned with the repair and maintenance of computer hardware, printers, and peripheral equipment. Compensation averages $15 to $25 an hour.

Office Professional. This job usually entails a variety of administrative responsibilities, depending on the number of employees and the size and complexity of the computer system. Daily duties may include: word processing, secretarial work, accounting, payroll preparation, graphics designing, and maintenance of personnel records. Salaries range from $25,000 to $45,000.

On-Line News Director. This website position is similar to that of a TV/radio news director or a newspaper managing editor. In addition to supervising reporters, photographers, and other news personnel, the news director may do writing, editing, interviewing and reporting. Salaries for on-line directors range from $25,000 at small websites to $100,000 or more at major Internet news centers.

On-Line Reporter. A website reporter gathers and writes news much like a television or print reporter. However, since most Internet news staffs are small, a web reporter also may have duties as a proofreader, copywriter, editor, columnist, even graphic artist. In markets of equal size, salaries for reporters average about the same as paid by television stations.

HIGH-TECH SCHOLARS

A growing number of colleges and universities are now offering degrees in computer-based communication. The Bachelor of Science degree in information technology emphasizes development and use of of computer-based knowledge and skills to answer expanding communication needs. Graduates with this degree can qualify for high-paying positions in information technology/information systems.

Students studying networking and communication systems learn to analyze the needs of organizations and build networks to meet those needs. Upon graduating they are qualified to be network or system administrators or microcomputer specialists.

Majors in information technology management are finding employment as systems analysts, database administrators, end-user support specialists, and information systems managers.

Students who complete courses in multimedia technology acquire competency in designing, developing, and implementing computer-based multimedia programs or web pages for clients in such fields as education, marketing, information, and entertainment.

WEBSITE BUSINESS

By 1998 some forty million adult Americans were estimated to be browsing the Internet with some regularity. On-line shopping is popular, especially with females, who comprise more than 40 percent of the Internet audience. Using "Push" technology, a growing number of web surfers are actively purchasing or subscribing for products, services, information, and entertainment offered on the Internet.

A survey by the Association of Retail Advertisers revealed that 90 percent of the nation's major retailers have websites and budget more each year for site maintenance, sales, advertising, and promotion. This can only mean plentiful career opportunities in the next millennium.

ON-LINE ENTREPRENEURS

After a Pittsburgh radio station changed formats and fired Ann Devlin, she originated a daily interview show on the Internet, and quickly found a sponsor. Members of her computer audience, who have the proper software, can listen to the program, transmit e-mail comments, view photos of the hostess and her guests, and even access the archives to view previous programs.

Another Internet pioneer, Scott Kaplan, hosts a weekly sports and comedy show at the CBS website in New York. Janice Malone originates a nightly Internet gossip program from her in-home Dallas studio. Other shows produced exclusively for web browsers deal with a multitude of subjects that computer owners like to read about and discuss. Individual marketers and established businesses are using the Internet to sell all kinds of products and to disseminate, without restrictions, advertising, publicity, and propaganda.

Though not expected to replace already-established media, the expanding worldwide web should continue to grow and make room for innovative and proficient communicators.

ELECTRONIC JOB FINDERS

Although direct face-to-face contact with an employer is usually the best way to apply for a job, this option isn't always available. Only after reading a letter of application, looking over a resume, or finding out about you in some other way is a hiring manager likely to grant you an interview.

One new and effective way to make yourself known is to rely on electronic employment resources. The Internet can give you access to numerous websites that provide job listings, job-hunting resources, and networking groups. Many employers actively search computer employment databases when hiring personnel.

More than a million job openings are now advertised on five-thousand Internet sites, according to John Sumser, editor of *Electronic Recruiting News*. He estimates that twenty to fifty new sites appear every day, many of them opened by major companies.

Applying for employment on the Internet demonstrates your familiarity with computers, and this can be helpful because computer experience is required to qualify for a growing number of jobs.

The Electronic Job Matching Database is a free service available to all job seekers, including broadcasters and journalists. They will use your resume to develop an electronic profile of your training and experience. To participate, send your resume to 1915 North Dale Mabry Highway, Suite 307, Tampa, Florida 33607; phone (812) 879-4100.

Numerous other electronic employment agencies charge a nominal fee, but it is an easy and relatively inexpensive way to reach and impress a large number of prospective employers with a single resume.

Complete information about how to job hunt on the Internet is available in *Electronic Job Search Almanac 1997,* published by Adams Media Corp.

INTERNET Q & A

After working successfully for sixteen years as a radio and television journalist, Richard Warner organized his own communication company, specializing in computerized information services.

The firm, What's Up, uses fax and Internet to distribute thousands of daily press releases. Staff members, many with extensive computer and broadcasting experience, also design, program, and maintain websites for numerous clients.

Here are Warner's answers to questions that students most often ask him about the Internet:

Q. How is the Internet likely to evolve?

A. Just as radio and television multiplied aural and visual options for consumers, hundreds of thousands of websites and news groups now offer an ever-expanding array of topics and choices. The Internet will not replace radio or TV, but it does vastly increase an individual's communication options.

Q. What career opportunities does the Internet offer?

A. It's hard to predict how the Internet job market will develop because computer technology and job requirements keep changing, but it's safe to say that certain positions in sales, content creation, graphic design, and computer programming will always be a fundamental part of the Internet business. The Internet will create both salaried and entrepreneurial opportunities. Because the web can be a "great equalizer," some will venture out, as I did, and create their own successful Internet services companies. Others will elect to work as employees of larger, established website organizations.

110   *Opportunities in Broadcasting Careers*

Q. How much money can I expect to make?

A. If you operate your own business, the amount of money you make will depend largely on your own skills and hard work. If you choose to work for someone else, computer programming specialists and salespeople appear to have the greatest earning potential. Pay for an entry-level programmer is modest, but a skilled, high-end programmer, right out of school, can command $35,000 to $90,000. The amount varies according to size of company and area of the country. Website salespeople usually earn $15,000 to $20,000 as beginners, but good ones quickly increase their earnings. Graphic artists start at $20,000 to $25,000, but those with higher animation skills are paid more. Writers and other content creators are not in as much demand because so much Internet editorial matter is created by outside news, public relations, and advertising sources. Jobs that are available usually start at $14,000 to $20,000.

Q. Should I concentrate on taking computer and web development courses in college?

A. While it is desirable to learn a lot about your chosen field of work, you should study a variety of other subjects. This will make your college experience more comprehensive and improve your chances of finding employment in another field if your interests or job opportunities should change.

Q. What do you foresee five or ten years from now?

A. I think we are going to see the worldwide web becoming a real vehicle of mass communication for advertising, information retrieval, news, and entertainment. Currently, the volume of growth is enormous. In short, the Internet will become as powerful and prolific as newspapers, magazines, TV, and radio are today.

CHAPTER 11

NONBROADCAST VIDEO SYSTEMS

Thousands of businesses and institutions have their own broadcasting studios and video systems that they use to create and transmit various kinds of programming to specific audiences at one or more locations. Company officials often appear on camera from national headquarters and address employees or stockholders in a number of cities. Simpler types of audio and video equipment are widely used to feed music, announcements, or visual presentations to multiple stores.

Former broadcasters often like working as managers, producers, and performers for these narrowcasting facilities because they provide good salaries, pleasant working conditions, job stability, and minimal worry about deadlines and audience ratings.

This expanding field of opportunity, often referred to as "corporate video," or "nonbroadcast video," has been likened to employment at a small-market television station. The audience is limited in size and so is the communication system. A few staff members handle many different duties. The director also may serve as scriptwriter, lighting engineer, and cameraperson. It's a splendid place to gain experience, and many young men and women advance from such jobs to bigger and better ones.

VIDEO SYSTEMS—BIG BUSINESS

Video systems employ far more people than all the radio and television stations in the United States and Canada. Owners of video systems include educational institutions, hospitals, government agencies, museums, independent producers, postproduction studios, and professional associations. Video systems productions run the gamut from feature-length movies and TV commercials to training films, slides, and sales promotion materials.

Corporate video employs more than 150,000 people. Independent producers account for at least another 75,000. The total number of personnel in all of the nation's video systems exceeds 500,000, so it is an inviting area to go job-hunting.

VIDEO SYSTEMS JOBS

Video Manager. The video manager is responsible for overall management of an audiovisual department. He or she approves staff and salaries. Qualifications are administrative and budgeting experience, and an up-to-date understanding of communication technology. Typical salary is about $50,000 to $60,000.

Supervisor/Operations Manager. This person supervises a media department or studio. He or she coordinates scheduling of audiovisual productions. The supervisor also recommends annual budgets, staff changes, and salary adjustments. Average salary is $40,000 to $50,000.

One-Person Operation/Video Coordinator. This multitalented individual handles all the creative, technical, production, and management responsibilities for a small facility. Salary range is $30,000 to $60,000.

Producer/Corporate Communication Representative. He or she coordinates all aspects of an assigned video production. The producer is responsible for determining the objectives to be achieved and assembling the necessary creative and technical personnel. The producer then oversees the project to complete it on time and within budget. Typical starting salary is $30,000; with five years' experience, $50,000.

Assistant Producer/Video Coordinator. He or she assists in carrying out all of the producer's objectives and duties. This person also may serve as a writer. Salary range is $20,000 to $30,000.

Director. The director selects and directs the talent and technical crew in creating an actual production on location or in a studio. Typical starting salary is $25,000.

Production Assistant. He or she assists the director in changing sets, adjusting lighting, revising scripts, or providing any other help that is needed. Salary range is $20,000 to $30,000.

Writer. A writer evaluates and interprets the client's needs, researches source materials, and develops scripts for production. Typical first-year salary range is $20,000 to $30,000.

Audio/Video Specialist. This person has a thorough knowledge of electronic media and is capable of setting up media programs and installations. He or she can also troubleshoot equipment problems. First year salary range is $25,000 to $30,000.

Engineer/Chief Video Specialist. An engineer is responsible for the technical performance of video and audio recording, switching, and distribution equipment. He or she installs, tests, and evaluates electronic devices and reviews new developments in equipment and techniques. Starting salary range is $25,000 to $30,000.

Technician. A technician serves as a technical member of an audio, video, or film crew. To qualify you must be capable of operating and maintaining electronic equipment. Typical starting salary is $20,000.

Videographer/Cameraperson. He or she operates a camera to record action on videotape and has knowledge of lighting and shot composition. A videographer sometimes produces and edits small-format video. Pay averages $15 to $20 an hour.

Sales/Marketing. Sales and marketing personnel are responsible for selling and marketing audio/video programs, products, or services. Typical first-year earnings are $25,000.

Professor/Instructor. A full-time teacher of electronic communications subjects may work at a college, university, or in a school system. Beginning salary range is $30,000 to $35,000.

VIDEO PRODUCTION

Commercial video production is a rapidly expanding business in the United States and Canada, generating more than $30 billion in revenues annually. The biggest share of this comes from producing spots and color graphics, but the output includes hundreds of different types of informational and entertainment presentations, everything from TV programs and feature films to brief commercial and public service announcements.

You will find dozens of video producers and video production studios listed in the phone books of most large cities, and they are numerous even in smaller communities. In addition, some 12,000 part-time operations in TV stations, cable systems, and various public and private organizations make this dynamic industry a large employer of skilled communicators.

Postproduction houses also are growing in number. They specialize in enhancing the aural and visual elements of a video presentation—voices, music, sound effects, titles, and graphics—to create the finished product.

Principal clients of postproduction houses are advertising agencies, contract producers, and corporations, which require assistance in completing TV commercials, feature films, music videos, and other audio-video presentations.

Most job opportunities in this field call for creative and artistic talent, plus a working knowledge of video-audio recorders, character generators, editing equipment, monitors, and computers. On-the-job training is the best way to gain such experience.

VIDEO PRODUCTION JOBS

Manager/Office Manager. A manager supervises the day-to-day operation of the production company and serves as the top administrator. In small operations, this person also may be the business manager/controller and may do some writing and production. He or she should combine creative and management capabilities and have a degree and experience in electronic media. Salary range is $50,000 to $100,000.

Administrative Assistant/Secretary. This person assists the manager with correspondence, community relations, record keeping, and overall supervision of personnel and operations. He or she may serve as bookkeeper-receptionist in small organizations and handle billings, payroll, and accounts receivable. The job requires a business school or college education and media experience. Typical salary is $30,000.

Sales/Marketing Manager. This manager develops and coordinates the company's sales and marketing efforts to obtain as many business clients as possible. He or she supervises the sales staff. In small operations, the marketing manager also may do writing and production. Requirements are a degree in marketing, advertising, or communications and media sales experience. Base salary range is $45,000 to $85,000.

Account Executive. An account executive makes sales calls to obtain new business and services existing accounts. A college degree is preferred, plus sales training and experience. Compensation is $30,000 to $75,000.

Marketing/Sales Assistant. He or she provides assistance to the sales manager and account executives. The job involves maintaining records of all business transactions and sales activity. To qualify you must be a high school graduate; a college degree is preferable. You should have sales potential with skills in math, computer operation, and general office work. Salary range is $20,000 to $35,000.

Production Manager. This person is responsible for all studio production and supervision of production staff. In small operations this job may include creative production duties. Requirements are a degree in communications and several years of TV production experience. Salary range is $45,000 to $90,000.

Producer/Director. He or she plans, develops, and directs video productions to meet the needs and specifications of individual clients—anything from fifteen-second TV commercials to feature-length made-for-TV movies. Requirements are a degree in broadcasting or theater and TV production experience. Salary range is $35,000 to $55,000.

Scriptwriter. A scriptwriter is responsible for transforming the client's wishes into a visually oriented script—including narration dialogue and camera instructions—and then making whatever changes, deletions, or additions are called for during production. The position requires a college degree and proven writing skills. Many writers work on a freelance basis and are paid by the assignment. A full-time scriptwriter usually doubles as a producer-director. Compensation range is $25,000 to $65,000.

Videographer. This person shoots and edits tape or film at a production studio, works under the supervision of a producer or director, and uses appropriate cameras, lenses, and lighting equipment. To qualify you should be educated and experienced in cinematography. Pay averages $20 to $40 an hour.

VIDEO POSTPRODUCTION JOBS

The following positions exist in postproduction facilities, where video presentations are edited into their final form, combining all of the visual and audio elements. These employees are generally recruited from TV stations or other production studios where they have gained experience with editing equipment and character generators.

Off-Line Editor. This person works in an editing suite and does the initial major editing of a videotape or film footage. Skilled video editors are in demand for both freelance work and full-time positions. Salary range is $40,000 to $75,000.

On-Line Editor. An on-line editor works with clients on editing a videotape production into its final form. He or she operates computers and technical machines to integrate and coordinate the desired visual and aural components. The job requires special skills and experience. Salary range is $40,000 to $85,000.

Assistant Editor. This person sets up editing machines and character generators for use by the editor. The assistant editor keeps track of reels and logs and provides help wherever needed. Salary range is $35,000 to $50,000.

Audio Engineer. This sound specialist does the final blending and balancing of voices, sound effects, and music into the finished video production. Prerequisites are technical training and audio-engineering experience. Pay range is $20 to $40 an hour.

Maintenance Engineer. He or she is responsible for keeping the studio's technical equipment in good working order. The job requires technical training and experience and problem-solving skills. Pay averages $15 to $20 an hour. Duplication engineers earn about $15 an hour.

Telecine Colorist. This person specializes in maximizing the color potential of a videotape production. He or she uses computerized equipment to equalize and enhance videotapes transferred from film and tapes of varying color intensity. The position requires a high degree of artistic and technical talent. Pay is good: $75,000 to $100,000, and sometimes more.

CHAPTER 12

BROADCAST-RELATED JOBS

Every year thousands of students at colleges, universities, and trade schools take courses in electronic communication. Many of them would like to be broadcasters, but they outnumber openings in the television, radio, and cable industries. Fortunately, however, they can usually find employment in other places where their skills are needed.

Knowledge of broadcasting has helped many students obtain good positions in advertising, marketing, fund-raising, promotion, publicity, and public relations. Electronic media specialists also are building successful careers by helping develop, sell, and distribute various video and audio products, including programs, games, and computer software. Many governmental, religious, cultural, and social service agencies hire communication experts to keep the public informed about their activities and provide leadership in fund-raising. So getting employed as an electronic media professional should be relatively easy, providing you are adequately prepared and willing to work in a broadcast-related field. A number of such jobs are described in this chapter.

SALES REPRESENTATIVES

Most commercial broadcasting facilities are affiliated with sales organizations that maintain offices in principal cities and sell out-of-town advertising time for their client stations. Sales representatives, commonly known as "sales reps," deal mainly with national and regional advertisers. To be a successful rep you should love to sell and do so in a smart, aggressive, and pleasing manner. Commissions and earnings are high for those who work long and hard, but competition for sales jobs is keen. Some rep firms engage in program production, own broadcast properties, and employ specialists in research, marketing, programming, and promotion.

ADVERTISING AGENCIES

The robust economy of the 1990s and the emergence of many new businesses have benefited not only all forms of advertising, but the media that transmit their commercial messages as well. Advertising growth has been especially strong in electronic media. Many of the nation's advertising agencies have prospered and created a favorable employment situation, with heavy recruitment of specialists in creative and account services. Job openings for media analysts and buyers are less numerous because computerization has reduced need for their services. Generally, however, agencies are doing well and expanding their involvement in marketing, sales promotion, direct response advertising, and interactive communication systems.

Approximately 170,000 men and women are employed by advertising agencies. Two-thirds of the firms they work for reported in 1998 that they are adding people to their payrolls or planning to do so. Many of the newly hired are selected because they have broadcast experience and are needed to help develop and place advertising and programming on radio and television stations, cable systems, and the Internet. Individuals with electronic communication skills also are being recruited to serve as account executives, copywriters, media directors, and specialists in marketing, merchandising, promotion, and public relations.

Advertising is expected to continue growing in the twenty-first century, with increased spending on media that offer customers a high degree of control, either through interactivity or greater choice of products and services. The highest percentage of ad growth is forecast for interactive digital media, on-line services, and subscription video, a category that includes cable TV, direct-broadcast satellite, and pay-per-view programming. All of this commercial activity should translate into continued growth of advertising agency jobs. Compensation for these positions has risen markedly in recent years. Most agencies augment salaries with annual bonuses. (See Table 12.1.)

Table 12.1 Ad Agency Compensation for Men and Women

Title	Average Base Pay (Men & Women)	Men Average	Women Average	Average Bonus	Total Compensation
C.E.O.	$148,600	$153,000	$154,200	$70,300	$218,900
Chief Operating Officer	128,300	134,800	112,500	45,600	173,900
Financial Manager	73,000	80,600	63,100	12,600	85,600
Creative Director	94,800	104,400	90,400	17,100	111,900
Art Director	50,100	51,000	44,700	4,400	54,500
Chief Copywriter	48,400	53,800	44,700	4,300	52,700
Media Director	56,700	63,000	52,800	6,600	63,300
Senior Account Executive	65,400	72,900	59,400	8,000	73,400
Account Executive	37,800	39,300	36,700	3,100	40,900

Source: AM & G survey conducted for *Advertising Age*, Dec. 1, 1997. Salaries are subject to skews due to small sample return from larger agencies.

Ad Agency Jobs*

Creative Director. Develops advertising and marketing concepts and campaigns and works with a staff of assistants to see them successfully produced. The job requires creative vision, understanding of sales and marketing psychology, and management skills. Salary range is $61,000 to $163,000.

Media Director. Identifies target audiences for advertising campaigns and determines what media to use to achieve desired results. Job requires experience in media analysis and planning. Salary range is $38,000 to $95,000.

Time Buyer. Purchases time periods for client's advertising messages on selected electronic media, using audience ratings, demographic and psychographic research, and good judgment. Salary range is $25,000 to $75,000.

Copywriter. Writes copy for video and audio commercials, utilizing innovative skills as an entertaining and persuasive promoter of a client's philosophy, product, or services. Salary range is $36,500 to $71,000.

Art Director. Creates and develops original and compelling methods of visually portraying advertising themes and sales messages. Must have proven artistic talent and graphic design experience. Salary range is $41,000 to $70,500.

Senior Account Executive. This position is held by experienced, top-level salespeople, who have a record of success in obtaining advertising clients and satisfying their needs. Although women are more numerous than men in this position, they make somewhat less money. Salary range is $56,000 to $82,000 for females; $64,500 to $96,000 for males.

Account Executive. Women outnumber men in this position, two to one. Responsibilities are similar to those of a senior account executive, but less experience is required. Salary range is $34,500 to $44,000 for females; $37,000 to $43,000 for males.

Research Director. This media-market analyst provides the ad agency and clients with advertising research findings and explains their significance. To qualify you must be educated in research techniques and procedures and be capable of initiating and conducting research projects or contracting for such studies. Salary range is $45,000 to $75,000.

---

*Sources: AM&G survey findings, *Advertising Age,* Dec. 1, 1997; and personal research, 1997–98, by the author.

ENTRY-LEVEL POSITIONS

Assistant Media Planner/Traffic Coordinator: $17,500 to $22,500
Assistant Account Executive: $20,000 to $25,000
Account Executive/Media Desk Coordinator: $27,500 to $32,500

PUBLIC RELATIONS

Employers frequently hire people with electronic media experience to fill public relations positions. This is understandable because basic channels of communication, such as radio, television, cable, and the computer Internet, are crucial conduits for reaching and influencing large numbers of people.

Richard Yarbrough majored in radio and television in college, then worked as a radio scriptwriter, salesperson, and president of a public relations firm before being named vice president–public relations, Bell South corporation. He later was drafted to head public relations for the 1996 Olympic Games. Now semiretired, he lectures frequently at the University of Georgia, emphasizing to students that public relations is not the same as publicity or promotion, but rather a counseling profession deserving of lifelong study and discipline. Yarbrough credits his early broadcast experience with teaching him many precepts that he has used as a PR professional.

Requisites for a public relations position include empathy, patience, and analytical ability; oral and written communication skills; familiarity with print, video, and audio practices and technology; and knowledge of history, political science, current events, public opinion, psychology, and demographics.

About 175,000 men and women hold accredited public relations jobs in the United States. Thousands more are employed in Canada. Compensation varies according to the size of the organization and responsibilities of the job. Salaries run from $25,000 to $250,000 and up.

PUBLIC INFORMATION

Most large public and private organizations employ one or more professional communicators to prepare and disseminate news and publicity releases, edit publications, reply to requests and questions from the public, and cultivate media contacts. The position, commonly known as a public information officer (PIO), requires communication skills and knowledge of journalism practices, publicity, and public relations. Applicants with electronic media education and experience are frequently favored for this job. Anyone who likes this type work and does it well can make it a launching pad to higher levels of management and compensation.

FREELANCE TALENT

A growing number of artists, craftspeople, writers, musicians, actors, and technicians work as talent for hire. Futurist Watts Wacker predicts that additional millions will make a living this way in the next millennium, freelancing for a variety of clients just as tradesmen did during the guild system of the Middle Ages. This is happening because computerized automation is shrinking payrolls and permitting companies to replace full-time employees with part-timers or temporaries.

One of the hottest growth areas for freelancers is in electronic media, but pay varies according to the experience and caliber of the talent. To command top dollar, you must consistently perform at a superior level. Some who have proved that it can be done are Regis Philbin, Kathie Lee Gifford, Tim Allen, Bill Cosby, Diane Sawyer, Montel Williams, and Maury Povich.

SYNDICATED PROGRAM SERVICES

In the United States there are at least 80 TV news services and a similar number of radio news services. More than 75 companies provide formatted programming to radio stations. At least 1,000 businesses inventory, produce, and distribute movies, programs, and features for TV, radio, and cable. In addition, some 35 pay-cable services, and an equal number of syndicators, sell sports programs and special events. Dozens of companies in Canada also produce and market various kinds of programs for radio, TV, and cable.

The output of these firms requires the creative and marketing efforts of many writers, directors, performers, technicians, and sales professionals. Opportunities exist for capable newcomers to join their ranks. Jobs are available in program development, production, and marketing. Organizations engaged in all types of programming and syndication are listed in the annual *Broadcasting/Cable Yearbook* and other similar publications.

VOICE OF AMERICA

The Voice of America (VOA) has responsibility for broadcasting around the world by radio to convey positive information about the United States and its people. Through newscasts, interviews, documentaries, commentaries, and special events coverage, effort is made to provide overseas listeners with accurate, objective information regarding American activities, government policies, and public opinion.

The VOA has a network of transmitters and relay stations in the continental United States and abroad. Broadcasts are transmitted on shortwave and medium-wave in forty languages. Inquiries about employment should be addressed to the Voice of America, 330 Independence Avenue, SW, Washington, DC 20547.

UNCLE SAM'S RADIO–TV

The Armed Forces Radio and Television Service (AFRTS) operates more than 700 radio and TV stations. They are located at military bases in 130 foreign countries, aboard navy ships at sea, and in remote areas where U.S. forces are stationed. Some are conventional broadcasting systems. Others are closed-circuit operations. Both military and civilian personnel work at these installations, and after gaining valuable experience, quite a few have become well-known radio and television personalities.

Some AFRTS stations share programming as members of a network. Others function independently and create most of their own programming. All radio and TV outlets are supplied a number of programs by the AFRTS Broadcast Center, March Air Reserve Base, California 92518-2017. To obtain job information contact The Armed Forces Radio and Television Service, 601 North Fairfax Street, Alexandria, Virginia 22314.

"FREE" RADIO

Radio Free Europe/Radio Liberty broadcasts to Eastern European countries in a number of languages and dialects. Radio Free Asia provides a similar broadcast service for Middle Eastern countries. Radio Marti and TV Marti transmit programs to Cuba. International Radio is a government-sponsored radio service for listeners in distant American provinces and territories. These broadcasting agencies are federally subsidized operations, designed to disseminate news and information about America and its allies that is not always available to people in other parts of the world. To obtain more details about these agencies and possible job openings, contact Radio Free Europe/Radio Liberty, 1201 Connecticut Avenue, NW, Washington, DC 20036.

NONPROFIT ORGANIZATIONS

Employment opportunities for specialists in radio, television, and Internet communication are plentiful among nonprofit organizations. Included in this vast panorama of enterprises are large numbers of charities and social service agencies, including medical research labs; educational institutions; and religious, governmental, social, and political-action groups. Altogether about a million organizations employ more than eight million people and disseminate billions of dollars annually, contributed by generous-hearted Americans. Many employees prefer to work for a nonprofit agency. There's usually less stress and competitive pressure than in a profit-making business, but salaries don't always match those paid in the private sector. For additional information read *Opportunities in Nonprofit Organizations,* by Adrian Paradis, NTC Contemporary Publishing Group, Lincolnwood, Illinois.

CHAPTER 13

JOBS FOR WOMEN AND MINORITIES

Employment opportunities in electronic media for women and minorities are gradually improving. More than 40 percent of all broadcasting and narrowcasting jobs are now held by females. Overall minority representation in the industry is nearing 30 percent. This indicates not only compliance with equal opportunity laws, but also growing awareness of the talent, versatility, and economic importance of America's diversified population. Broadcasters report general satisfaction with minority employees, both male and female, most of whom are "dependable, hardworking, and loyal."

This is no doubt why so many stations now employ women as supervisors and managers. Almost two-thirds of all television producers and nearly half of the assignment editors are females, who are highly prized for their judgment, coolness under fire, and interactive leadership qualities.

The handicapped also are finding more opportunities in electronic media companies. Technology has reduced physical requirements for many jobs, permitting professionals with disabilities to qualify for a variety of positions. If you fall into this category, don't hesitate to apply for work in some area of broadcasting or narrowcasting.

This is not to imply that all employers will welcome you with open arms. Regrettably, some organizations are still slow and reluctant to hire women, ethnic applicants, or disabled persons. Although Congress and the FCC have decreed that licensees of commercial or noncommercial radio, TV, and cable systems must offer equal employment opportunity to all qualified persons, they have not entirely eliminated prejudicial hiring practices.

But Will Wright, African-American news director of WWOR-TV, Secaucus, New Jersey, has found "a lot more fairness and compassion among broadcasters than in any other industry," and he's encouraged to see a growing number of minorities entering the ranks of management and ownership.*

THE MINORITY SUCCESS ROUTE

A common complaint among broadcasters in smaller communities is the difficulty they have in attracting qualified personnel, especially minority personnel. Many newcomers to the profession apparently want to work only in major markets and choose to be unemployed unless they can find the high-salaried position they have in mind.

If the only job available pays a modest salary and is in a small market, you should accept it and work hard to excel at it. This beats being idle. Besides, working in a small or medium-sized community offers certain advantages. Very likely you'll be able to gain a wealth of practical experience that you can use to further your career. This is the route that many minority professionals have followed to become managers or owners of broadcasting facilities.

So don't be reluctant to start at the bottom, and think twice before leaving a job prematurely to accept another that pays a few more dollars. Take time to get acquainted with the organization you work for. Study how it operates. Learn as much as you can about the organization's management philosophy and commercial practices. As you gain experience and demonstrate your worthiness, other offers may come your way. You may decide to make a move if it fits with your career objectives. On the other hand, you may choose to stay where you are or start your own communication business.

Several Asian-Americans pooled their resources and built KPST-TV, Vallejo, California, which they still own and operate. A group of Hispanic broadcasters started XEWT-TV, to provide Spanish-language programming for viewers in the San Diego area. Dorothy Brunson and Willie Davis, both African-Americans, have done well at buying and operating radio properties. Al Roker, a minority star on the, NBC *Today* show, owns a TV-Internet production company.

Doors of opportunity in broadcasting and narrowcasting are opening for newcomers of all races and ethnic groups who are professionally prepared and determined to succeed.

Tables 13.1 through 13.4 show the position of minorities in radio-TV, cable TV, broadcast news, and local broadcast news.

---

*Sources: FCC Industry EEO Report, 1997; RTNDA *Communicator*, August, 1996; and personal interviews conducted by the author.

Table 13.1 Minorities in Radio-TV

Position	# of Employees	Black FEMALE	Black MALE	Hispanic FEMALE	Hispanic MALE	Asian FEMALE	Asian MALE	Native American/Alaskan FEMALE	Native American/Alaskan MALE
Officials/Managers	4,145	1,000	905	691	915	213	164	116	141
Performers	9,206	2,237	2,355	1,239	2,072	589	361	138	215
Technical	6,050	657	2,457	264	1,969	111	417	38	138
Sales	3,180	767	732	681	631	146	80	83	60
Clerical	5,807	2,568	333	1,935	323	419	66	142	21
Craftspeople	224	9	36	15	121	4	27	4	8
Operatives	221	10	67	14	113	1	6	5	8
Laborers	97	7	21	4	5	1	3	0	2
Services	281	36	125	20	85	0	13	0	2
Totals	29,211	7,291	7,031	4,863	6,234	1,484	1,137	526	595

Source: Equal Employment Opportunity Trend Report, prepared for FCC Industry EEO Unit, July 4, 1997.

Table 13.2 Minorities in Cable TV

Position	# of Employees	Black FEMALE	Black MALE	Hispanic FEMALE	Hispanic MALE	Asian FEMALE	Asian MALE	Native American/Alaskan FEMALE	Native American/Alaskan MALE
Officials/Managers	2,466	656	704	325	450	89	110	40	92
Performers	667	200	130	108	105	52	46	13	13
Technical	3,820	193	1,863	88	1,156	45	354	7	114
Sales	2,908	894	943	318	511	65	128	25	25
Clerical	14,148	7,188	1,500	3,568	915	493	200	235	49
Craftspeople	2,881	73	1,487	29	1,952	11	155	4	107
Operatives	5,358	134	2,663	62	1,052	22	380	7	138
Laborers	319	19	157	10	110	0	17	1	5
Services	87	6	33	4	40	0	3	0	0
Totals	32,654	9,363	9,480	4,512	6,291	777	1,393	332	543

Source: Equal Employment Opportunity Trend Report, prepared for FCC Industry EEO Unit, July 4, 1997.

Table 13.3 Broadcast Racial Composition–News

	TV	Radio	TV News Director	Radio News Director	TV News Anchor	TV Sports Anchor
Caucasian	81%	88%	91%	91%	81%	89%
African-American	9%	6%	1%	5%	11%	5%
Hispanic/Latino	6%	4%	4%	2%	4%	4%
Asian-American	3%	1%	2%	1%	3%	2%
Native American	1%	1%	2%	1%	1%	0%

Source: RTNDA/Ball State University survey; reported in *Communicator*, August 1996.

Table 13.4 Women and Minorities in Local Broadcast News (Full-Time Employees)

	Television	Radio
News Staffs with Women	96%	31%
Women News Directors	17%	26%
Women News Anchors	54%	N/A
Women News Reporters	51%	N/A
Women News Producers	64%	N/A
News Staffs with Minorities	81%	13%
Minority News Directors	9%	9%

Source: RTNDA/Ball State University survey; reported in *Communicator*, August 1996.

GENDER SALARY COMPARISON

Although the salary gap between male and female employees is narrowing, a 1997 survey conducted by Women in Cable and the Telecommunications Foundation showed that female professionals in cable, DBS, and wireless cable companies average earning $50,378, while males holding similar jobs average $59,354. Entry-level salaries for women is $26,064, only 3 percent less than for men. Differences in pay are more pronounced at upper management levels. Women supervisors in cable average earning $31,860, about 25 percent less than men. Similar but smaller gaps of 10 percent to 11 percent are common in radio, TV, public relations, and advertising.

Table 13.5 Gender Salary Comparison

Job (entry-level)	Male Salary	Female Salary	Difference
Professional/Technical	$26,779	$26,034	−2.8%
Associate Professional/Technical	$29,902	$31,133	+4.1%
Director	$80,254	$71,448	−11%
Manager	$53,502	$44,607	−17%
Officer	$105,831	$92,438	−11%
Senior Officer	$136,804	$121,817	−12.7%

Source: Women in Cable/Telecommunications Foundation survey, 1997.

MINORITY BROADCAST OWNERSHIP*

Although the FCC does not require broadcast licensees to identify their race or ethnicity, the Minority Telecommunications Development Program in the Department of Commerce annually collects information from various periodicals and other sources regarding minority ownership of radio and television stations.

As of January 1, 1998, minorities owned an estimated total of 322 commercial broadcast properties, representing 2.8 percent of all the stations in the country. African-Americans comprise the largest group of minority broadcasters, with ninety-eight black owners controlling 193 radio and television licenses, Hispanic ownership totaling 120 stations, Asian-Americans having 4, and Native Americans owning 5.

Table 13.6 Minority-Owned Commercial Broadcast Stations in the United States 1997

Type Station	Black	Hispanic	Asian	Native American	Totals	Percentages
AM	101	80	1	2	184	3.8%
FM	64	31	2	3	100	1.8%
TV	28	9	1	0	38	3.2%
Total	193	120	4	5	322	2.8%

*Source: Survey Findings of The Minority Telecommunication Development Program, U.S. Department of Commerce, 1997.

Since passage of the Telecommunication Act of 1996 and relaxation of ownership rules by the FCC, group owners are buying large numbers of stations, including some that are minority owned. This may account for evidence of decline in minority ownership. Other factors may be lack of access to investment capital and not enough legislation and policy initiatives to encourage minorities to buy broadcast properties.

BROADCAP

As a means of encouraging minority entrepreneurs to buy and operate radio and television stations, the broadcast industry established the nonprofit Broadcast Capital Fund (BROADCAP) in 1978. Since then this organization has played a major role in increasing the number of minority-owned AM, FM, VHF, and UHF stations from 40 to nearly 300.

Applicants for BROADCAP assistance generally fall into three categories: 1. persons who have worked in minority-owned facilities and have been recommended by their employers; 2. minorities with construction permits who need financial assistance in building their stations; and 3. individuals who have succeeded in some other profession but want to become broadcast owners so they can serve the needs and interests of the minority community.

BROADCAP President Anthony L. Williams hopes that with the coming of digital communication and the auctioning of electronic magnetic spectrum by the FCC, even more minorities will seize the opportunity to become owners of electronic communication facilities.

To obtain more information about BROADCAP, write or call Broadcast Capital Fund, Inc., 1700 K Street, Suite 405, Washington, DC 20006.

NEW OPPORTUNITIES

Although consolidation of station ownership is eliminating some radio and TV jobs, it also is creating quite a few new ones. Instead of working for one radio or TV station, you may qualify to represent a group of stations as an account executive or a specialist in news, programming, production, marketing, engineering, or research. Multiple-station owners are encouraging intermarket programming, syndication purchases, and the creation of mininetworks and special events. Qualified people are being selected for these high-salaried positions. "Look at what your solid skills are and how they translate into any media environment," advises Sheryl Mimford, who heads the California Bay Area Broadcast Skills Bank. This applies to all electronic media professionals—men, women, and minorities.

MINORITY VOICES AND CHOICES*

Gwen Ifill, African-American, political analyst, NBC News: "My father taught me to assume I have no limits; anything is possible."

Rick Diaz, Hispanic, news director, KRGF-TV, Weslaco, Texas: "Keep hanging in there and don't wait to be asked. Keep bringing up story ideas. Keep punching. You can't wait for it to come to you. You've got to go after it."

Robin Roberts, African-American, host of *Wide World of Sports* on ABC-TV: "As women progress in the athletic realm, it gives us more credibility as sports broadcasters. I can't imagine not having played sports, even at the college level, and trying to do what I'm doing."

Spencer Christian, African-American, ABC-TV weatherman and newscaster: "Read as much as you can and become a generalist. Learn a little about everything—current events, history, literature—because there's so much in news reporting that needs to be put into historical perspective."

Paula Walker, African-American, news director, WNBC-TV, New York: "I never wondered *whether* I'd get to this point in my career, just *when*. I always felt that I could go as far as I was able to go—given the opportunity."

Steve Majors, biracial news director, WFTS-TV, Tampa, Florida: "I can't claim I've ever been discriminated against, although some may patronize you because you're a minority or pander to you...Never think that you have arrived, because this business is about change. There are always new experiences and new opportunities."

FEMALE ROLE MODELS*

If you are female and seeking employment, don't anticipate being discriminated against or given special consideration. Just concentrate on getting your foot in the door so you can demonstrate your capabilities. Women have proved that they are able to handle any and all kinds of electronic communi-

---

*Source: Personal interviews by the author.

cation responsibilities and have earned the right to go job hunting with optimism and lofty ambitions.

This is how Lynn Andrews worked her way up to become president of the ABC radio network. The same is true of Frances Preston, president-CEO of Broadcast Music Inc.

Women now outnumber men on the sales and news staffs of many television, radio, and cable operations. Many managers prefer to hire females for these jobs because they tend to be "energetic, enthusiastic, adaptable, and well-organized."

After winning awards and a solid reputation as an aggressive reporter and clearheaded editor, Michelle Kornes was promoted to news director at WTOP, Washington, DC.

Katie Couric, Connie Chung, Roz Abrams, Ricki Lake, and Deborah Norville all learned the basics of broadcasting by doing menial tasks at hometown radio and TV stations.

Judy Woodruff's prominence as one of the nation's top news personalities resulted from many years of training and hard work, beginning with cub reporting at local TV stations. Paul Raymon, a former boss at WAGA-TV, Atlanta, recalls Woodruff as imaginative, resourceful, and destined for success.

Gayle King achieved so much popularity and respect as a news anchor and reporter at WFSB-TV, Hartford, Connecticut, that she was asked to create and host her own nationally syndicated talk show. She accepted with the stipulation that the daily program must originate in Hartford, so she could continue reporting news. That is real dedication.

Kathie Lee Gifford offers this advice to young women who would like to match her success in electronic communication: "Be patient. Do your best on every task you undertake. Try to gain as much knowledge and experience as you can. Make every opportunity work for you. If you're always looking forward to what's in the future, you'll never learn today what you need to learn. If you want to go straight to the top too fast, you're never going to have the foundation you need to stay on top."

When asked what factors are critical in achieving success, a group of prominent women broadcasters named the following: appearance, attitude, willingness to assume responsibility, enthusiasm, communication and organizational skills, cooperative spirit, lofty goals and objectives, loyalty, friendliness, and determination to win.

CHAPTER 14

THE MULTIMEDIA FUTURE

The world is moving rapidly into a multimedia age where methods of communication—TV, cable, radio, computers, even telephones and fax machines—speak a common language and rely on digital technology to transmit aural and visual information rapidly. Consequently, electronic sights and sounds in the twenty-first century will be quite different from anything previously transmitted.

Receivers in homes and offices—with monitors from palm-size to screens that cover an entire wall—will be interactive, permitting two-way "virtual reality" communication in vivid, three-dimensional color and high-fidelity stereo, relayed without distortion via fiber optic cable or satellite.

Cable companies throughout the country will provide subscribers with phone service, Internet access, free e-mail, more and varied programming, and numerous other useful features.

Businesses and households are destined to make widespread use of computers and TV sets in their professions. Laptop computers, and some even smaller, will become as common as briefcases. Instead of commuting to an office or workplace, large numbers of people will conduct business affairs from their homes and depend on digital devices to access, transmit, and share data and information. This may result in organizations holding fewer out-of-town meetings and engaging in more video conferences.

Many futurists predict that affordably priced communications technology will effect universal changes in commerce, industry, government, education, and all of our social institutions. Bran Ferren of Walt Disney Imagineering foresees the Internet transforming the world by touching hearts and minds of people everywhere. "Don't blow it by not believing it," he warns. "If we can get it right, we might be able to ensure a bright future for our children, which ought to be our highest goal." In any case, this expanding electronic environment should produce numerous promising career choices.*

THE CHANGING WORKPLACE

By the year 2005, government reports indicate that 150 million Americans will be in the workforce, but many will not be permanent employees of just one company. Instead, the average worker will switch jobs seven or more times before retiring. Don Lee, vice president of Right Management Consultants, predicts that preparing for a job or career will become less important than "preparing for the continuing development of skills, experiences, attitudes, and behavioral styles needed to accomplish what is really important to us."

Compensation will be based on results, with many of the highest earners being self-employed professionals who maintain at-home headquarters and depend heavily on what futurist George Gelder calls "The Teleputer"—a device that combines the capabilities of computer, TV, cable, phone, and fax—to carry out daily work assignments. Interactive digital devices also will be used increasingly for shopping, paying bills, banking, ordering groceries, conversing, and exchanging correspondence. As more ways to utilize new communication equipment emerge, jobs in the multibillion-dollar electronic media industry should multiply.

NARROWING THE FOCUS

While mass-market broadcasting has declined somewhat in popularity, interest in smaller-market narrowcasting has intensified. There is growing awareness among radio and TV professionals that money can be made by focusing on specific ethnic, generational, cultural, and professional audiences, each with its own interests and loyalties. Stations in a number of cities are catering to minority groups within the general population, developing programs and services to satisfy their particular wants and needs.

Numerous networks and syndicators are producing video and audio fare expressly for viewers and listeners of varying ages, incomes, and educational

---

*Source: Fidler, Roger. *Mediamorphosis—Understanding New Media.* Pine Forge Press, 1997.

levels. Quantities of programs are being designed for, and transmitted to, school students, sports fans, history buffs, music lovers, game players, and people whose primary interest is news, public affairs, comedy, art, religion, health, show business, or some other specialized subject.

WHAT'S ON THE HORIZON?

Consider the following:

- convergence of TV, radio, and computer technology
- consolidation of print, audio, and video techniques
- networks of interconnected electronic media systems
- electronic newspapers, magazines, and books
- videophone service in homes and businesses
- video conference centers
- video classrooms and colleges
- expanded pay-per-view movies, concerts, sports, and special events
- video-on-demand services
- inexpensive video paging and data services
- many more cable channels, networks, and program choices
- high-definition, three-dimensional, digital, virtual-reality TV
- digital FM and AM radio
- in-home multimedia centers
- Internet global marketing
- multiple usage of computers for buying, selling, advertising, and marketing; sending and receiving messages; two-way communication and participation; playing games; accessing libraries; watching TV shows; listening to music, paying bills, and obtaining unlimited amounts of information and entertainment
- interactive computer, cable, TV, and radio systems
- increased use of satellites and fiber optic cable
- better and smaller cameras
- digital recording and editing equipment
- smarter and more powerful computers

These are only some of the developments that are already available, or will be in the near future. Opportunities will be plentiful in this vast new electronic universe. To capitalize on them, the most valuable asset you can offer an employer is your ability and willingness to be consistently energetic, resourceful, and dependable. You should be capable of moving confidently from one job or assignment to another without difficulty or complaint. If you can meet the demands of tomorrow's new technology, you should achieve success.

DIGITAL TELEVISION

Under rules adopted by the FCC, America's TV stations will all eventually change from analog to digital broadcasting systems. This will be a gradual process, beginning with stations in the nation's largest markets. Because of heavy expenses involved in buying new digital equipment and hardships that the conversion process is expected to create, it will be well into the twenty-first century before nationwide digital television becomes a reality.

Some TV stations already have digital-equipped studios, and many radio and TV stations are using digital machines for recording, editing, billing, traffic and inventory control, program automation, in-house artwork, and news operations. As broadcasters find additional uses for computers, it should create a demand for more employees.

DIGITAL RADIO

The FCC envisions AM-FM radio stations in the United States changing from analog to digital audio systems, but it has not set a timetable for this to be done. Digital radio will equalize the power and audio quality of stations, providing all of them with interference-free, high-quality signals.

Digital technology is being used in radio stations for the handling of programming, production, sales, traffic, accounting, research, and news. The efficiency of digital devices has made it possible to automate many functions and operate with fewer employees.

A typical radio station in the twenty-first century will belong to a company that owns a large number of FM and AM outlets. It will have a relatively small staff, with each employee handling multiple duties. Radio performers will commonly work under contract. There will be fewer news personnel and news reports except on all-news or news-talk stations. Traffic and weather reports in the morning and afternoon drive time will likely be shared in a pool with other local stations. Many music stations will be automated and use preprogrammed music and features supplied by an outside source.

Eddie Fritts, president of the National Association of Broadcasters, foresees a bright future for radio because of its flexibility, consolidation, and efficiency.

MEGACHANNEL TELEVISION

The concept of a limited television spectrum is steadily evolving into a megachannel universe. Video compression and fiber optics are expanding the capacity of cable systems, making it possible to accommodate additional networks, programs, and services. Systems that previously offered 30 channels are increasing their menu to 40, 50, or 60. Some optimists envision cable systems with 500 channels. Of course, adding channels results in creating a large number of slivered audiences. This, in turn, may lead to a loss of advertisers. The maximum number of channels that a system can profitably accommodate has yet to be decided. But the expanding channel concept is sure to keep growing. This should increase employment opportunities for program developers, salespeople, technicians, and professionals in promotion, research, and marketing.

SATELLITE PROSPECTS

Satellites represent a window of growing opportunity for beginners in broadcasting because they are becoming a major player in global communication. Rotating in orbit high above the earth, satellites serve a multitude of TV and radio networks, stations, cable systems, and individual home and business subscribers. Direct broadcast satellite (DBS) systems beam programming to more than six million backyard or rooftop antennas in the United States, primarily to homes that do not have access to a cable system.

The full impact of DBS on other electronic media has yet to be felt, but the industry is healthy and is attracting customers by the quantity, quality, and variety of its video and audio services.

TOMORROW'S INTERMEDIA WORLD*

Will the Internet eventually replace media competitors? It's doubtful. Matt Miller, president of the Association of Independent Commercial Producers, contends that no medium that the public wants and needs ever has been replaced by another. For years people have predicted that newspapers, radios, and magazines would wither away, but they are still here, and many are prosperous. Instead of new media displacing older ones, Miller believes they will "work in concert," to serve various needs and purposes.

Instead of resisting the expansion of computer technology and growth of the worldwide web, print, radio, television, and cable all have embraced the Internet and are using it to sell and promote their own products and services.

For beginners in electronic media, the good news is that electronic media cooperation is creating an active job market.

OUTLOOK FOR STUDENTS

Whether you are going to college, a trade school, the armed forces, or directly into the electronic media workplace, you will need training and aptitude in the use of sophisticated communication devices. Employers are requiring job seekers to be computer literate and technically adept. To achieve your maximum potential you also will need a well-rounded education that exposes you to significant historical and current ideas and teaches you how to comprehend and communicate what you see, hear, and observe.

Students who are unable to leave home can use computers and cable connections to take courses, plug into library resources, and participate in classroom discussions. Thousands are presently doing so, including quite a few who are physically impaired.

Wherever you locate—in an academic setting or elsewhere—concentrate on increasing your knowledge and technical capabilities. Look for better ways to do things. Remember, the challenges that lie ahead may appear awesome, but so are the possibilities. In this age of remarkable new communication technology, those who are best prepared will reap the greatest rewards.

---

*Sources: Marian Salzman, "Riding with Technology to Millenium," *Advertising Age,* Oct. 7, 1997. "Worldwide Web," *Broadcasting & Cable,* Aug. 11, 1997. National Cable Television Association Research, 1997. Forrester research, 1997. Georgia Tech research, 1997. FCC Report No. 97-8, "Mass Media Action," April 3, 1997.

A FINAL WORD

Just as the public has accepted and utilized radio, TV, cable, and other electronic media for enlightenment and entertainment, so will it doubtlessly patronize other methods of audiovisual communication as they become available. This should translate into numerous career opportunities for persons capable of using both new and existing technology to interpret what is happening in commerce, science, medicine, show business, law, ecology, politics, domestic and international affairs, the arts, outer space, and dozens of other areas.

With the entire universe as their workplace, a new generation of broadcasters and narrowcasters will have unlimited subject matter to explore and exploit. Major topics that cry for insight and attention include the exploding world population; our deteriorating environment; broken families and neglected children; the drug crisis; crime and corruption; overcrowded cities; the economy; terrorists, and the threat of war; and the never-ending needs and problems of the sick, poor, hungry, and homeless.

Despite scientific advancements that have greatly magnified our ability to reach and inform people, no comparable breakthrough has occurred in the art of communication. That still requires a consistent and sincere human effort to understand others and make oneself understood.

In order to speak clearly and constructively about significant issues and ideas, communicators in the future will have to be better educated, more sensitive, and more resourceful than their predecessors. They must be sincerely dedicated to serving the needs and interests of the public and acutely conscious of their responsibility to be relevant, dependable, and fair.

It is hoped that such serious responsibilities and bright possibilities will entice you to become an electronic media professional and join the ranks of tomorrow's communication leaders.

APPENDIX A

SCHOLARSHIPS, GRANTS, AND LOANS

Anyone who is contemplating a career in electronic media should include a college education as necessary preparation. Help-wanted ads for broadcasters and narrowcasters frequently specify that applicants must have a degree in communication plus professional experience.

Although attending an institution of higher learning has become quite expensive, this need not keep you from earning a degree. Thousands of students are receiving financial aid through outright grants, loans, and work-study programs.

FEDERAL ASSISTANCE

Low-interest loans from the federal government are available to parents of college-bound students, regardless of income or resources. Applicants must file a Free Application for Federal Student Assistance (FAFSA) form. High school students should check with their school's financial aid office to obtain application forms and deadline dates. This office also can provide information about other sources of federal, state, and private aid that may be available.

OTHER AID SOURCES

Public and private organizations also offer a variety of student loans and scholarships. In the state of Georgia, for example, any high school graduate who maintains an acceptable grade average is eligible to receive a free

"Hope" four-year college scholarship. Contact your state department of education to find out what kinds of financial assistance are available.

HOW TO GET A LOAN

Information about student loans and other forms of financial aid can be obtained from:

Academic Management Services
50 Vision Boulevard
P.O. Box 14608
East Providence, RI 02914

Some colleges require an independent assessment of a family's financial situation before granting a student a loan. Two organizations that offer this service are:

ACT Student Assistance Programs
2255 North Dubuque Road, Box 168
Iowa City, IA 52243

College Entrance Examination Board
425 Columbus Avenue
New York, NY 10023

FINANCIAL AID REFERENCES

The following volumes provide helpful information for students who need financial aid to further their education:

Cassidy, David J. *The Scholarship Book.* Paramus, NJ: Prentice-Hall, 1996.
College Students' Guide to Merit and Other No-Need Funding. El Dorado, CA: Reference Service Press, 1996–1998.
Directory of Financial Aids for Women. El Dorado, CA: Reference Service Press, 1997–1999.
The Journalist's Road to Success—A Career and Scholarship Guide. New York: Dow Jones Newspaper Fund, Inc., 1996.
Scholarships, Fellowships and Loans. Detroit: Gale Research, 1997.
The Student Guide (Gives details about federal assistance programs.) To obtain a copy, contact your school's financial aid office or call (800) 4-FED-AID.
Sumner, David E. *Graduate Programs in Journalism and Mass Communications.* Iowa State University Press, 1996.

INTERNET STUDENT AID SOURCES

The worldwide web offers information about financial aid for students at numerous websites. These are four principal ones:

FinAid—The Financial Aid Information Page
http://www.finaid.org/finaid.html

This comprehensive page links to fastWEB, the scholarship research service, and other sources, including the U.S. Department of Education's Student Guide (current edition). It is available by clicking on "US Government Info" and then "student guide."

fastWEB
http://www.fastweb.com

Financial Aid Search Through the WEB (fastWEB) is a free scholarship search program where you can set up a personal profile to receive details of scholarships and awards related to your skills and abilities. Accessing fastWEB also will enable you to set up a mailbox for receiving additional updated information.

College Board Online
http://www.collegeboard.org/index.html

This website provides much helpful advice for college-bound students about financial aid and includes a college search program.

Department of Education
http://www.ed.gov/offices/OPE/

This home page for the Department of Education can link you with numerous information sources for students and parents. FAFSA Express (provider of applications for Federal Student Financial Assistance) may be accessed from this website or at *http://www.ed.gov/offices/OPE/express.html*

ASSISTANCE FOR MINORITY STUDENTS

College Fund-UNCS (formerly United Negro College Fund)
120 Wool Street, 10th Floor
New York, NY 10005

LULAC National Education Service Center
1133 Twentieth Street NW, Suite 750
Washington, DC 20036 (include self-addressed stamped envelope)

National Hispanic Scholarship Fund
1 Sansome Street, Suite 1000
San Francisco, CA 94104

National Scholarship Service and Fund for Negro Students
250 Auburn Avenue, Suite 500
Atlanta, GA 30303

GRANTORS OF MEDIA SCHOLARSHIPS

Asian American Journalists Association
1765 Sutter Street, Suite 1000
San Francisco, CA 94115

Broadcast Education Association
c/o National Association of Broadcasters
1771 N Street NW
Washington, DC 20036

Corporation for Public Broadcasting
901 E Street NW
Washington, DC 20004

Dallas–Ft. Worth Association of Black Communicator Scholarships
Communication Center
400 South Record Street
Dallas, TX 75202

Gannett Foundation
1101 Wilson Boulevard
Arlington, VA 22209

The Hearst Foundation
90 New Montgomery Street, Suite 1212
San Francisco, CA 94105

Institute of Electrical and Electronic Engineers
345 East Forty-seventh Street
New York, NY 10017

Radio and Television News Directors' Foundation
  1000 Connecticut Avenue NW, Suite 615
  Washington, DC 20036

Residential Fellows Program
  Media Studies Center
  580 Madison Avenue, 42nd floor
  New York, NY 10022

Scripps Howard Foundation
  P.O. Box 5380
  Cincinnati, OH 45202

Society of Broadcast Engineers
  8445 Keystone Crossing, Suite 140
  Indianapolis, IN 46240

APPENDIX B
SUGGESTED READING

GENERAL REFERENCE

Broadcasting & Cable Yearbook, issued annually. Cahner's Publishing Co. Standard reference for radio, television, cable, and allied arts.

Bryant, J. Black and S. Thompson. *Introduction to Media Communication,* 5th edition. New York: McGraw-Hill, 1997.

Camenson, Blythe and Jan Goldberg. *Real People Working in Communications.* Lincolnwood, IL: NTC/Contemporary Publishing Group, 1997.

Dertouzous, Michael. *What Will Be: How the New World of Information Will Change Our Lives.* New York: HarperCollins, 1997.

Doyle, Mark. *The Future of Television—A Global Overview of Programming, Advertising, Technology and Growth.* Lincolnwood, IL: NTC/Contemporary Publishing Group, 1994.

Jankowski, Gene F. and David C. Fuchs. *Television Today and Tomorrow.* New York: Oxford University Press, 1995.

Orlik, Peter B. *The Electronic Media: An Introduction to the Profession.* Iowa State University Press, 1997.

CAREER GUIDANCE

Bone, Jan. *Opportunities in Telecommunications Careers.* Lincolnwood, IL: NTC/Contemporary Publishing Group, 1995.

Eberts, Marjorie and Margaret Gisler. *Careers for Computer Buffs & Other Technological Types.* Lincolnwood, IL: NTC/Contemporary Publishing Group, 1997.
Electronic Job Search Almanac 1997. Holbrook, MA: Adams Media Corporation, 1997.
Glossbreaner, Alfred. *Finding a Job On the Internet.* New York: McGraw-Hill, 1995.
Goldberg, Jan. *Great Jobs for Computer Science Majors.* Lincolnwood, IL: NTC/Contemporary Publishing Group, 1997.
Noronha, Shonan F. R. *Careers in Communications.* Lincolnwood, IL: NTC/Contemporary Publishing Group, 1995.
Pattis, S. William. *Careers in Advertising.* Lincolnwood, IL: NTC/Contemporary Publishing Group, 1996.
Rotman, Morris E. *Opportunities in Public Relations Careers.* Lincolnwood, IL: NTC/Contemporary Publishing Group, 1995.
Stair, Lila B. *Careers in Computers.* Lincolnwood, IL: NTC/Contemporary Publishing Group, 1997.

CHANGING TECHNOLOGY

Ditingo, Vincent A. *The Remaking of Radio.* Woburn, MA: Focal Press, 1997.
Fidler, Roger. *Mediamorphosis—Understanding New Media.* Thousand Oaks, CA: Pine Forge Press, 1997.
Gilster, Paul. *Digital Literacy.* New York: John Wiley & Sons, Inc., 1997.
Hart, Ann. *Cyberscribes.1—The New Journalists.* San Diego, CA: Ellipsys International Publications, Inc., 1997.
Wittle, David B. *Cyberspace: The Human Dimension.* New York: W.H. Freeman & Co., 1997.

MULTIMEDIA PERIODICALS

Advertising Age
   Crain Communications, Inc.
   744 Rush Street
   Chicago, IL 60601

   Advertising industry weekly. Includes ads for jobs.

Broadcasting & Cable
  Cahners Publishing Co.
  1735 DeSales Street NW
  Washington, DC 20036

  Weekly journal of activities in TV, cable, radio, satellite, and computer industries. Numerous job listings.

Cable Communications Magazine
  Ter-Sat Media Publications
  1421 Victoria Street
  Kitchner, Ontario N2B 3B8
  Canada

  Monthly coverage of cable TV in Canada and elsewhere.

Cablecaster
  Southern Magazine Group
  1450 Don Mills Road
  Don Mills, Ontario M3B 1X7
  Canada

  Coverage of the Canadian cable industry. Published eight times a year.

Communications Daily
  Warren Publishing, Inc.
  2115 Ward Court, NW
  Washington, DC 20037

  Daily electronic-communication news service. Available on-line.

Electronic Media
  Crain Communications Inc.
  740 Rush Street
  Chicago, IL 60611

  Daily and weekly issues cover electronic media, including help-wanted ads.

Multimedia Monitor
  Future Systems Inc.
  Box 26
  Falls Church, VA 22040

  Monthly coverage of worldwide multimedia techniques and applications.

RTNDA Communicator
Radio and Television News Directors Association
1717 K Street, NW
Washington, DC 20037

Monthly devoted to all facets of electronic news coverage.

Satellite Week
Fortuna Communications Corporation
Box 308
Fortuna, CA 95540

News of the satellite communications industry.

Television Quarterly
National Academy of Television Arts and Sciences
111 West Fifty-seventh Street, Suite 100
New York, NY 10019

Interpretation of television events, trends, and progress.

TV Guide (U.S. and Canadian regional editions)
Murdock Magazines—Four Radnor Corporate Center
100 Matsonford Road—Box 500
Radnor, PA 19088

Weekly coverage of TV and cable shows, personalities, and program schedules.